# עַם יִשְׂרָאֵל חַי

# Celebrating Israel in Our Lives

## Shalom Orzach

Edited by Ari Y. Goldberg

United Synagogue of Conservative Judaism
Department of Youth Activities

# THE UNITED SYNAGOGUE OF CONSERVATIVE JUDAISM DEPARTMENT OF YOUTH ACTIVITIES

Jules A. Gutin, *Director*
Gila R. Hadani, *Assistant Director*
Marsha B. Goldwasser, *Activities Coordinator*
Marc Louis Stober, *Publications Coordinator*
Karen Stein, *Education Coordinator*
Rachel Field, *Projects Coordinator*
Ze'ev Kainan, *Central Shaliach*
Yitzchak Jacobsen, *Director, Israel Office*
David Keren, *Director of USY Programs, Israel*

## NATIONAL YOUTH COMMISSION

Marshall Baltuch, *Chairman*
Jonathan S. Greenberg, *Education Committee Chairman*

## THE UNITED SYNAGOGUE OF CONSERVATIVE JUDAISM

Stephen S. Wolnek, *President*
Rabbi Jerome M. Epstein, *Executive Vice-President*

A publication of the National Youth Commission,
United Synagogue of Conservative Judaism
155 Fifth Avenue, New York, New York  10010

First Edition, 1998

Cover design by 21st Century Publishing and Communications
Manufactured in the United States of America

# Table of Contents

Introduction..................................................................................................1

**Chapter 1: Eretz Yisrael in the Texts**................................................................3
    Go Forth From Your Land
    The Importance of Living in Israel

**Chapter 2: Jerusalem - An Echo of Eternity**.................................................11

**Chapter 3: The Essence of Jerusalem**............................................................19

**Chapter 4: Zionism 101 - Introduction to the Critical Thinkers and Doers**..........25
    Rabbi Abraham Isaac Kook
    Ahad Ha'am
    Theodor Herzl
    A.D. Gordon
    Hatikvah: Israel's National Anthem

**Chapter 5: Between Tel Aviv and New York - Two Promised Lands**.........................39
    The American Dream
    The New Jew
    Here to Stay by Hillel Halkin

**Chapter 6: Israel's Declaration of Independence**............................................49

**Chapter 7: What is the State of the Jews**.......................................................57
    The Status Quo Letter
    The Law of Return
    Reflections

**Chapter 8: The Jewish People - Dare We Be One**............................................69

**Chapter 9: Will the Real Israeli Please Stand Up**...........................................73
    Ultra Orthodox
    Religious Nationalist
    Secularist
    New Immigrant

**Conclusion: Shnat Hayovel - Back to the Future**...........................................79

# Acknowledgments

I wish to thank my good friends and colleagues at Melitz, specifically Pinchas Zimmer for their guidance and encouragement. I would also like to express me deep felt respect and appreciation to Steven Sachs who helped with much of the research for this volume.

I wish to dedicate this sourcebook to my parents who continue to instill me with a love for Israel and the Jewish People. My passion for Jewish Education is due to their example. I thank my wife, Stephanie, and our three boys, Yossef, Aviad, and Yishai for their patience and support. Their comments and feedback can be found throughout this work.

Shalom Orzach

---

This volume has benefited from the combined wisdom and experience of the talented individuals who read the manuscript of this book. I am indebted to them for their constructive comments and suggestions:

Rabbi Jerome M. Epstein
Jules A. Gutin
Gila R. Hadani
Yitzchak Jacobsen
Ze'ev Kainan
Rabbi James M. Lebeau
Marilyn Sladowsky
Karen Stein

In particular I would like to express thanks to Jules Gutin for his important contributions to the questions and exercises in this book, and to Gila Hadani, who has been a valued partner during the development of this sourcebook. To my wife, Stacy, and daughter, Rina, I extend my love and appreciation for another year of their understanding and support. Memories of our year in Israel have been a special source of inspiration.

Ari Y. Goldberg

# INTRODUCTION

וקדשתם את שנת החמשים שנה וקראתם דרור בארץ לכל ישביה יובל הוא תהיה
לכם ושבתם איש אל אחזתו ואיש אל משפחתו תשבו.

*And you shall make holy the fiftieth year, and proclaim liberty throughout the land
for all its inhabitants. It shall be a Jubilee for you: each of you shall return to his
holding and each of you shall return to his family. (Vayikra 25:10)*

The Fiftieth Year, the "*Yovel,* " of the State of Israel carries with it a sense of history, the
enormity of which is humbling. We have merited living in an age where a Jewish homeland
is a reality and is taken for granted. Only sixty years ago more than half of the Jewish world
were stateless, refugees searching for a home.

The prayers and dreams of millions of Jews since the destruction of the Second Temple
have been answered. The establishment of the Jewish State has transformed the Jewish
People from being footnotes in the history of others to being writers and players in their
own self written and ongoing history.

In 1896 Theodor Herzl, the father of political Zionism, wrote in the *Jewish Chronicle*, the
prestigious Jewish Weekly of British Jewry;

> "*I am introducing no new idea, on the contrary it is a very old one. It is a
> universal idea and therein lies its power, old as the people which never, even in
> the time of bitterest calamity, ceased to cherish it. This is the restoration of the
> Jewish State.*"

This notion of a Jewish State is to a great extent reflected in Herzl's Book *Altneuland* (Old
New Land).

For many people Zionism was not just a reaction to anti-Semitism, but was a belief in the
messianic prophecy and the historic destiny of the Jewish People.

Today that tension is played out on the streets of the modern State of Israel. It is my hope
that this sourcebook will enliven these very debates and will, in so doing, invite not only
more opinions, but also suggestions.

Shalom Orzach.
September 1998.

# Chapter 1
## Eretz Yisrael in the Texts:  Biblical, Midrashic, Prayer and Modern

Few subjects in our tradition have been given so much attention as the continuous relationship between the Jews and Israel. It fills the pages of our literature and liturgy. Almost every Jewish life cycle event has a reference to Zion. It is as if from the very beginnings of the exile, after the destruction of the second Holy Temple, we were conditioned to live with Israel even though, or perhaps because, we were without it.

As we begin to briefly delve into some of these texts, we will sense very quickly the essential role that Israel has always played in our religious identity, in our understanding of ourselves, and in our understanding of the world around us.

## Our Ties to *Eretz Yisrael* Through the Eyes of the Torah and Rabbinic Literature

<u>Go Forth From Your Land</u>

ויאמר ה אל אברם לך לך מארצך וממולדתך ומבית אביך אל הארץ אשר אראך.

*And God said to Abram, go forth from your land and from your birthplace, and from your father's house, to the land that I will show you: And I will make of you a great nation, and I will bless you, and make your name great . . .* (Bereshit 12:1-2)

This is the first mention in the Torah regarding the connection between the Jewish People and the land of Israel.

To fully appreciate the significance of this passage it is important to look at it in its own context and to attempt to understand the process that led to this event.

In essence there were three fundamental stages in the development of the Jewish People up to that point in our history, as related by the stories in Bereshit - the Book of Genesis.

> I.   The creation of humanity
> II.  The generation of the flood; here the process of creation began again with Noah and his three sons
> III. Abraham and his descendants

Clearly there was a process of spiritual evolution concerning the creation of the Jewish People. That is, it is only through very specific personalities or families that our heritage is traced. This is clearly illustrated through the events and trials that Abraham was asked to fulfill, and it is here that we can understand the role that Israel was to play in his development.

The command that Abraham received was somewhat strange in that it involved:
(1) leaving his land,
(2) leaving his birthplace, and
(3) leaving his parents.

4

**Put yourself in Abraham's place and think about which of these three places would be the most difficult to leave. Explain your answer.**

_____

_____

_____

_____

**Which of these three places affects your beliefs the most? the least? How and why?**

_____

_____

_____

_____

You would expect that the order of these three things would be the opposite. That is, a person leaves his parents, his birthplace, and then perhaps his land. In fact, there is great significance to the order that God chose. A person is affected very directly by his or her parents, character, genes, etc. A person is affected to a somewhat lesser extent by immediate family, and even less by his or her society (i.e., nature/nurture). Therefore, the significance of the order of the command given by God to Abraham was, in fact, to make it easier for Abraham to obey the command.

The command begins with the words _"lech lecha"_ - go forth for yourself. Abraham should go to <u>himself</u>. In order to do so he had to separate himself from all the influences that had affected <u>his</u> development. Hence, the first stage was for Abraham to leave his land, his society. Comparatively, this was the easiest challenge since the society was the least important in directly influencing Abraham's development. The second stage - family, was understandably more difficult, and then ultimately stage three - father or parents - was the most difficult. Therefore, the demand God made on Abraham was to separate from all the influences: biological, psychological, as well as cultural.

**Complete the following sentence: "My connection to Israel is_____**

_____

The following passages are taken from Midrashic sources, and some from the Talmud. They reflect a phenomenal commitment and attachment to Israel. The earlier sources were written not long after the destruction of the Second Temple, and one can almost sense the pain of the writers and the fact that they surely missed home.

ת"ר: לעולם ידור אדם בא"י אפי' בעיר שרובה עובדי כוכבים, ואל ידור בחו"ל ואפילו בעיר שרובה ישראל. שכל הדר בארץ ישראל - דומה כמי שיש לו אלוה, וכל הדר בחוצה לארץ - דומה כמי שאין לו אלוה.

*Our rabbis taught: One should always live in Eretz Yisrael even in a city where the majority are non-Jews, and not live outside the Land even in a city where the majority are Jews. Whoever lives in Eretz Yisrael is as one who has God while whoever lives outside Eretz Yisrael is as one who has no God. (Ketubot 110b)*

מוטב ללון במדברות של ארץ ישראל ולא בפלטיות של חוצה לארץ.

*It is better to spend the night in the wilderness of Eretz Israel than to spend the night in palaces outside Eretz Israel. (Bereshit Rabbah 39)*

מעשה בר' יהודה בן בתרא ור' מתיא בן חרש ור' חנינא בן אחי ר' יהושע ור' יונתן שהיו יוצאים חוצה לארץ והגיעו לפלטוס וזכרו את ארץ ישראל זקפו עיניהם וזלגו דמעותיהם וקרעו בגדיהם וקראו המקרא הזה: וירשתם אתה וישבתם בה ושמרתם לעשות את כל החקים. וחזרו ובאו למקומם אמרו ישיבת ארץ ישראל שקולה כנגד כל המצות שבתורה.

*The story is told of R. Yehuda ben Beteira and R. Matya ben Heresh and R. Hanina ben Ahi, R. Yehoshua and R. Yonatan. They were traveling from the Land, arrived at a place named Platus, and remembered Eretz Yisrael. They turned their eyes toward it [Eretz Yisrael] and wept. They tore their garments and recited this verse: "You shall inherit and dwell therein, and you shall observe all the laws." They returned home and concluded: Dwelling in Eretz Yisrael outweighs all the commandments of the Torah. (Midrash Sifrei Reeh)*

Prof. Gerson Cohen once observed: "The rabbis could no more conceive of Judaism without the land of Israel than they could have [conceived of Judaism] without the people of Israel." They were not able to imagine God arranging things in any other way.[1]

**Describe how you think Judaism would be different today without Israel.**

_____

_____

_____

דרש רבי שמלאי: מפני מה נתאוה משה רבינו ליכנס לא"י?
וכי לאכול מפריה הוא צריך? או לשבוע מטובה הוא צריך? אלא כך אמר משה: הרבה מצות
נצטוו ישראל ואין מתקיימין אלא בא"י. אכנס אני לארץ כדי שיתקיימו כולן על ידי.

*R. Simlai expounded: Why did Moses so desire to enter Eretz Yisrael? Did he need its fruits or its bounty? No - this is what Moses said: "There are many mitzvot that Israel has been commanded which can be fulfilled only in the Land. Permit me to enter that I too may fulfill them personally."* (Sotah 14a)

[2]Living in *Eretz Yisrael* was considered so important that Jewish law permitted things that would normally have been prohibited in order to enable settling in *Eretz Yisrael*. For example, although writing and conducting business is strictly forbidden on Shabbat, the rabbis held that if one was acquiring a house in *Eretz Yisrael* one could write out the bill of the sale on *Shabbat*. (Bava Kamma 80b).

In another example, if a man living outside the Land wanted to make *aliyah* but his wife refused, she must either reconsider and go with him or receive a divorce and forfeit payment of her marriage contract. The same rule applied to a couple living in *Eretz Yisrael* if one of them wanted to leave: the law supported the one remaining in the country. In Rabbinic times, leaving *Eretz Yisrael* was deemed a religious infraction

---

[1] As quoted in: Simcha Kling, *The People and Its Land* (New York, United Synagogue Youth, 1988), page 33.

[2]The remainder of this chapter is adapted from *The People and Its Land*, pages 36-37.

Whether the Jews actually had freedom in their own land or had to live under the rule of a conqueror, whether they were allowed to dwell in *Eretz Yisrael* or were forced into exile, the Jewish People have never surrendered their claim to Israel. Based upon God's promise to Abraham in the Book of Bereshit, we are convinced that God had chosen us for the Land of Israel.

כי כל הארץ אשר אתה ראה לך אתננה ולזרעך עד עולם.

*I give all the land that you see to you and your offspring forever.* (Bereshit 13:15)

The rabbis insisted that even just studying about the *mitzvah* of settling in *Eretz Yisrael* is of prime importance, and it is enhanced when practiced in the Holy Land itself.

אין תורה כתורת ארץ ישראל ואין חכמה כחכמת ארץ ישראל.

*There is no Torah like the Torah of Eretz Yisrael and no wisdom like the wisdom of Eretz Yisrael.* (Sifrei Ekev)

## Questions for Thought

1. How do you think that the verses from *Lech Lecha,* relating the command that Abram received to go forth from his land, affects the Jewish people's connection to the Land of Israel?

2. How do you think the place where you live influences the way you live Jewishly?

3. Why do you think so much importance was put on living in the Land of Israel?

4. The concept of *pikuah nefesh* is that any Jewish law may be transgressed in order to save a human life. Are you aware of any other circumstances where Jewish law permits what is ordinarily forbidden? What status does this give to the commandment of living in the Land of Israel?

5. Do you agree or disagree with the Midrashic statement that "dwelling in Eretz Yisrael outweighs all the commandments of the Torah?" Explain why you feel this way.

6. Which is better: to live in Israel and obey no Jewish rituals, or to live in North America as a traditional Jew? Why?

7. How significant is it today to claim that we were promised the Land of Israel in the Bible? Does that statement weaken or strengthen our claim to the Land.

## Exercise

Imagine that you decided to make *aliyah*. When you told your parents they were very upset with your decision and they felt that you were abandoning your family and were not being sensitive to their feelings by not first discussing it with them. Furthermore, they begged you to reconsider your decision. What do you tell your parents about your reasons for wanting to make *aliyah*?

_____

_____

_____

_____

_____

_____

# Chapter 2
## Jerusalem: An Echo of Eternity

Until this point, we have sensed a relationship between the Jewish people and Israel both as a place and as a concept. Indeed, this was the basis of one of Dr. Abraham Joshua Heschel's classic works - Israel: An Echo of Eternity. But when it comes to Jerusalem this connection takes on incredible proportions.

On the two most emotional moments of our annual Festival cycle, at the close of the Pesah Seder and at the very end of the prayers of Yom Kippur, we pledge "Next Year in Jerusalem" - לשנה הבאה בירושלים

Our daily prayers, as well as *Birkat HaMazon* - Grace after Meals - are full of references to Zion and Israel, and specifically Jerusalem. The *Amidah,* recited three times a day, is said while facing Jerusalem. There is hardly a moment where Jerusalem is not mentioned and brought into our collective memory. The sources that follow attempt to throw some light onto the mystery pervading this city.

# Jerusalem: The Holy City

Jerusalem - the very name excites and stirs emotions, memories and glimpses of the past. Even when the Jews were dispersed, we never abandoned our dream of returning to Zion. The sources below attempt to enlighten us about this city that binds the Jewish People in an eternal bond with it.

## The World - Like the Human Eye
*The world is like the human eyeball: the white of the eye, these are the oceans surrounding the world; the black, this is the dry land; the pupil, this is Jerusalem; and the lens, this is the Temple, may it be speedily rebuilt in our days!* (Derech Eretz Zutah 9:26)

## The City That Unites
*"Jerusalem built up, a city knit together"* (Tehillim 122:3) - *the city that unites all Jews in companionship.* (Jerusalem Talmud, Hagigah 3:6)

## All Who Pray in Jerusalem
*All who pray in Jerusalem pray, as it were, before the Throne of Glory, for Jerusalem is the gate to heaven that is ever open to prayer.* (Pirke de-Rabbi Eliezer 35)

## Jerusalem's Beauty

עשרה קבים חכמה ירדו לעולם. תשעה נטלה ארץ ישראל. ואחד כל העולם כולו.
עשרה קבים יופי ירדו לעולם. תשעה נטלה ירושלים. ואחד כל העולם כולו.

*Ten measures of wisdom descended to the world - nine were taken by Eretz Yisrael and one by the rest of the world. Ten measures of beauty descended to the world - nine were taken by Jerusalem and one by the rest of the world.* (Kiddushin 49b)

## Jerusalem's Glory

מי שלא ראה ירושלים בתפארתה לא ראה כרך נחמד מעולם.

*He who has not seen Jerusalem in its glory has never seen a beautiful city.*
(Sukkah 51b)

## A Light Unto the Nations
*In time to come Jerusalem will become as a torch unto the nations of the world, and they will walk in its light.* (Pesikta Rabbati)

## Remembering Jerusalem

*Every Jew has to promise to go and live in the Land of Israel and to yearn for the privilege of praying there before God's sanctuary. Even though it is destroyed, the Divine Presence has not left it. So hear me, brothers and friends, remember Jerusalem ... and do not, Heaven forbid, think of settling outside the Land. It seems to us that as soon as we enjoy some tranquillity outside the Land of Israel, it is as though we have found another Land of Israel and another Jerusalem, and that is why all these evils have come upon us.* (Rabbi Jacob Emden, 1745)

## Two Brothers

*On the site where the Temple stood, two brothers once lived. The elder did not marry, and was all alone in the world. The younger had a wife and three children. The brothers had no material possessions except a plot of land which they had inherited from their father. They did not want to divide up the land, because they loved each other. Instead, they worked the land together, and when the harvest was over they counted the sheaves and divided them equally between them, placing them in two piles, each beside his own tent.*

*One year, after the harvest, the elder brother lay down to sleep beside his pile. But he could not fall asleep, because the thought ran through his mind: My brother has a wife and children to care for, while I am alone in the world and I work only to fill my belly. It isn't right that I should take an equal share with my brother. At midnight he got up, took some sheaves from his pile and placed them on his brother's pile. Then he returned to his place and slept peacefully. That same night the younger brother was also unable to sleep. He thought: My brother is all alone in the world. I have sons who will look after me when I am unable to work. What will my brother do in his old age? It isn't fair to me to take an equal share of the produce of our field! So before daybreak, the younger brother got up, took a few sheaves from his pile, stealthily placed them on his brother's pile and slept.*

*In the morning, the brothers saw that their piles were as large as ever. They wondered greatly about this, but they did not say a word to each other. The same thing happened the next night and the morning that followed. On the third night, as the brothers were carrying sheaves to each other's piles, they met midway, recognized each other, and wept, for they realized what had been happening. They left their sheaves on the spot where they had met, and without a word returned to their respective tents. God saw what the brothers had done, and He blessed the spot where they had met. Later, Solomon, King of Israel, built the Temple on that very spot - the Temple from which the message of peace, love and brotherhood went out to the whole world.* (an ancient legend)

## The Wedding in Jerusalem

*In betrothal contracts written in the home of Rabbi Levi Isaac of Berditchev, it was stipulated: "The wedding will, God willing take place in the Holy City of Jerusalem. But if, Heaven forbid, because of our sins, the Messiah will not have come by then, the wedding will take place in Berditchev."* (a Jewish folktale)

## Travelers to Jerusalem

*I am writing you this letter from the Holy City of Jerusalem . . . What can I tell you about the country? Great is the misery, and great the devastation, and, in brief, the more sacred the place, the greater the desolation; Jerusalem is more devastated than the rest of the country, and Judah more than Galilee; but in spite of its desolation the Land is good.*

*There are about 2,000 inhabitants, including about 300 Christians, refugees who escaped the sword of the Sultan; but there are no Jews. For after the arrival of the Tatars the Jews fled and some were killed by the sword. There are now only two brothers, dyers, who buy their dyes from the government. At their place, a quorum of worshipers meets on the Sabbath. And we encouraged them and found a ruined house, built on pillars and with a beautiful dome, and made it into a synagogue; for the town has no ruler and whoever wishes to take a ruin, can do so. And we volunteered to restore the building, and they have already begun and sent to the city of Nablus for the Scrolls of the Law which had been in Jerusalem, but were taken away when the Tatars came. And now they have established a synagogue, where they will pray. For people regularly come to Jerusalem, men and women, from Damascus and from Aleppo, and from all parts of the country, to see the Temple and weep over it. And may He Who has deemed us worthy to see Jerusalem in her ruins grant us to see her rebuilt and restored and the honor of the Divine Presence returned. And may you, my son, your brothers and your father's house, all be worthy to witness the good of Jerusalem and the comfort of Zion.* (Nahmanides' letter to his son, 1267)

## A People Which Mourns 2000 Years

*It happened once that Napoleon was passing by a synagogue on the Ninth of Av, at the time when the worshipers were sitting on the floor reciting elegies and weeping. "Why are they weeping?" he asked. They explained to him that they were weeping for their country which was destroyed nearly 2000 years ago. The explanation made a profound impression on the French emperor, who said: "A people that mourns and weeps for the loss of its homeland 2000 years and does not forget - such a people will never be destroyed. Such a people can rest assured that its homeland will be returned to it."* (folktale)

## The Redeemer Will Come

*The Tzechinover Rabbi Abraham was accustomed every year to come to the synagogue on the Ninth of Av with a new copy of the Elegies [lamenting the destruction of the Holy Temple] in his hands. He used to recite the Elegies, and when he had finished he would leave the book in a box under the lectern. When asked the reason, he used to say: "I am sure that next year the Redeemer will come to redeem us from exile and restore us to Jerusalem - so we will no longer need to recite the Elegies." (Hasidic tale)*

## The Way of Redemption

*Rabbi Hiyyah Rabba and Rabbi Simeon ben Halaffta were talking alone, one morning when dawn broke. Rabbi Hiyyah said to Rabbi Simeon: "That is how the Redemption of Israel will come about, at first little by little, and then the more light there is, the more it will increase and spread forth." (Jerusalem Talmud, Berachot 1)*

## For Zion's Sake

*For the sake of Zion I will not be silent, for the sake of Jerusalem I will not be still, until her victory emerge resplendent and her triumph like a flaming torch . . . Upon your walls, O Jerusalem, I have set watchmen, who will never be silent by day or by night. (Isaiah 62:1,2)*

## Ingathering of the Exiles

*Jerusalem will be built only when the exiles have been gathered in. So if someone tells you that all the exiles have returned, but Jerusalem has not yet been built, do not believe him, for it says (Tehillim 147:2): "The Lord rebuilds Jerusalem . . . " and only after that comes: "He gathers in the exiles of Israel." (Tanhuma, Noah, 11)*

Although this is a contemporary poem, written after the 1967 war, it is included in this chapter of traditional sources because of its prose about Jerusalem's history.

## THE PARATROOPERS CRY
By Haim Hefer, Translated by Michael Graetz

*This Wall has heard many prayers*
*This Wall has seen the fall of many other Walls*
*This Wall has felt the touch of mourning women*
*This Wall has felt petitions lodged between its stones.*
*This Wall saw Rabbi Yehuda Halevi trampled before it*
*But this Wall had never seen paratroopers cry.*

*This Wall saw them tired and wrung out*
*This Wall saw them wounded, mutilated*
*Running to it with excitement, cried, and silence*
*And creeping as torn creatures in the alleys of the Old City*
*As they are covered with dust and with parched lips*
*They whisper "If I forget thee, if I forgot thee, Jerusalem"*
*They are swift as eagles and strong as lions*
*And their tanks - the fiery chariots of Elijah the Prophet*
*They pass by with noise*
*They pass by as a stream*
*They remember the two thousand awful years*
*In which we had not even a Wall to place our tears before -*
*And here they stand before it and breathe in dust*
*Here they look at it with sweet pain*
*And tears run down and they look at one another perplexed.*

*How does it happen that paratroopers cry?*
*How does it happen that they touch this wall with great emotion?*
*How does it happen that their weeping changes to song?*
*Perhaps because these boys of nineteen, born at the same time as the state,*
*Perhaps because these boys of nineteen carry on their shoulders two thousand years.*

16

## Questions for Thought

1.   How do you account for so many references to Jerusalem in our traditional texts?

2.   What feeling do you get for the city of Jerusalem from these texts?

3.   "The City That Unites" says that Jerusalem unites all Jews in companionship. Is Jerusalem really a city of brotherhood in our day? Has it ever been? Similarly, would you consider the city of Jerusalem to be "A Light Unto the Nations"?

4.   The statements from "Jerusalem's Beauty" discuss 10 measures of wisdom and beauty which descended to the world. What do you think is meant by "wisdom" and "beauty" being taken by Israel and Jerusalem respectively? Is this at all literal?

4.   What is the moral of the story of the "Two Brothers?"

5.   "A People Which Mourns 2000 Years" relates Napoleon's positive impression to the Jewish people's strong commitment to its homeland. How do you think the Jewish people managed to keep such a strong connection to the land, despite being exiled from it for nearly 2000 years?

6.   What does Jerusalem mean to you?

## Exercise

Imagine that you are one of the young Israeli soldiers who liberated the Western Wall during the 1967 war. Write a letter to your grandparents in North America expressing your feelings at participating in that historic event. Especially keep in mind the final verse of Haim Hefer's poem - *"Perhaps because these boys of nineteen carry on their shoulders two thousand years."*

_____

_____

_____

_____

_____

_____

_____

# Chapter 3
## The Essence of Jerusalem

*"All streams flow into the sea, yet the sea is never full . . . "* (Kohelet 1:7) - *All of Israel never comes together except in Jerusalem, and they come up several times a year on the pilgrimage festivals - but Jerusalem is never really filled.* (Kohelet Rabbah 1)

Our Rabbi's explain that among the miracles performed in the Holy Temple during the three Pilgrimage Festivals, when many Jews flocked to the Holy City, was that no pilgrim ever complained that it was too crowded to find a place to lodge in Jerusalem. Another miracle that is mentioned occurred in the Temple itself, where everyone in the services found sufficient room to prostrate themselves despite the fact that they were standing very close to one another.

The Gaon of Vilna put forward a very enlightening explanation of this miracle. In reality Jerusalem and the Temple were very crowded, and that the miracle did not so much relate to the physical space getting larger, but the fact that nobody expressed discomfort or complained. Everyone showed love and friendship to one another and accepted the tight conditions with joy. There was, in a sense, a consensus that Jerusalem belonged to everyone equally (as in fact it does, since this area of Israel was intentionally not split among the 12 tribes).

What the Gaon of Vilna is highlighting is that the very essence and nature of Jerusalem caused this love and companionship between people. This idea is echoed by a statement in the Jerusalem Talmud: [Jerusalem is] *a city that in its very being makes all of Israel into friends.* (Hagiga 3:6).

The text suggests that the city creates friendship between its inhabitants. It is a city that makes *chaverim*.

On the following pages very similar themes are portrayed in the poetry of Yehuda Amichai, a well-known modern Israeli Poet.[1] These poems allow us to examine the complex characteristics of this magical city. Amichai seems to follow a tradition developed in Midrashic and Talmudic sources which implies that Jerusalem intrinsically has elements of holiness.

The poems (and sources) encourage us to grapple with the question of what essentially creates this aura of holiness. Do events and appropriate behavior give the city its identity and characteristics or are they intrinsic, and hence independent, and as such effect us? The Amichai poems invite this very discussion.

## ECOLOGY OF JERUSALEM

1     *The air over Jerusalem is saturated*
       *with prayers and dreams*
2     *like the air over industrial cities.*
3     *It's hard to breathe.*

4     *And from time to time a new*
       *shipment of history arrives*
5     *and the houses and towers are its*
       *packing materials.*
6     *Later these are discarded and piled up*
       *in dumps.*

7     *And sometimes candles arrive instead*
       *of people.*
8     *and then it's quiet.*
9     *And sometimes people come instead of*
       *candles.*
10     *and then there's noise.*

11     *And in enclosed gardens heavy with*
       *jasmine*
12     *foreign consulates.*
13     *Like wicked brides that have been*
       *rejected.*
14     *lie in wait for their moment.*

הָאֲוִיר מֵעַל לִירוּשָׁלַיִם רָווּי תְּפִלּוֹת וַחֲלוֹמוֹת
כְּמוֹ הָאֲוִיר מֵעַל לְעָרֵי תַּעֲשִׂיָּה כְּבֵדָה.
קָשֶׁה לִנְשֹׁם.

וּמִזְמַן לִזְמַן מַגִּיעַ מִשְׁלוֹחַ חָדָשׁ שֶׁל הִסְטוֹרְיָה
וְהַבָּתִּים וְהַמִּגְדָּלִים הֵם חָמְרֵי אֲרִיזָתָהּ,
שֶׁאַחַר כָּךְ מְשַׁלְּכִים וְנֶעֱרָמִים בַּעֲרֵמוֹת.

וְלִפְעָמִים בָּאִים נֵרוֹת בִּמְקוֹם בְּנֵי אָדָם,
אָז שֶׁקֶט.
וְלִפְעָמִים בָּאִים בְּנֵי אָדָם בִּמְקוֹם נֵרוֹת,
אָז רַעַשׁ.

וּבְתוֹךְ גַּנִּים סְגוּרִים, בֵּין שִׂיחֵי יַסְמִין
מְלֵאֵי בֹּשֶׂם, קוֹנְסוּלְיוֹת זָרוֹת,
כְּמוֹ כַּלּוֹת רָעוֹת שֶׁנִּדְחוּ,
אוֹרְבוֹת לִשְׁעָתָן.

## Questions for Thought

1. In line 3, why do prayers and dreams make it harder to breathe?

2. In lines 4-6, what are some examples of "shipments of history?"

3. Are all "shipments" discarded or do we keep some of them?

4. In lines 11-14, what moment are the foreign consulates waiting for?

## JERUSALEM IS FULL OF USED JEWS

1     *Jerusalem is full of used Jews, worn out by history,*

2     *Jews secondhand, slightly damaged, at bargain prices.*

3     *And the eye yearns toward Zion all the time.*

4     *And all the eyes of the living and the dead*

5     *are cracked like eggs on the rim of the bowl,*

6     *to make the city puff up rich and fat.*

7     *Jerusalem is full of tired Jews,*

8     *always goaded on again for holidays, for memorial days,*

9     *like circus bears dancing on aching legs.*

10    *What does Jerusalem need? It doesn't need a mayor,*

11    *it needs a ringmaster, whip in hand,*

12    *who can tame prophecies, train prophets to gallop*

13    *around and around in a circle, teach its stones to line up*

14    *in a bold, risky formation for the grand finale.*

15    *Later they'll jump back down again*

16    *to the sound of applause and wars.*

17    *And the eye yearns toward Zion, and weeps.*

יְרוּשָׁלַיִם מְלֵאָה יְהוּדִים מְשֻׁמָּשִׁים בְּהַסְטוֹרְיָה,
יְהוּדִים יַד שְׁנִיָּה, עִם פְּגִימוֹת קַלּוֹת, זוֹלִים יוֹתֵר.
וְהָעַיִן לְצִיּוֹן צוֹפִיָּה כָּל הַזְּמַן. וְכָל הָעֵינַיִם
שֶׁל חַיִּים וְשֶׁל מֵתִים נִשְׁבָּרוֹת כְּמוֹ בֵּיצִים
עַל שְׂפַת הַקְּעָרָה לַעֲשׂוֹת אֶת הָעִיר
עֲשִׁירָה וּשְׁמֵנָה וְתוֹפַחַת.

יְרוּשָׁלַיִם מְלֵאָה יְהוּדִים עֲיֵפִים
וְהֵם מְצֻלָּפִים תָּמִיד מֵחָדָשׁ לִימֵי זִכָּרוֹן וְחַג
כְּמוֹ דֻּבִּים מְרַקְּדִים בִּכְאֵב רַגְלַיִם.

מַה יְרוּשָׁלַיִם צְרִיכָה? הִיא לֹא צְרִיכָה רֹאשׁ עִיר,
הִיא צְרִיכָה מְנַהֵל קִרְקָס, עִם שׁוֹט בַּיָּד
לְאַלֵּף נְבוּאוֹת וּלְאַמֵּן נְבִיאִים לִדְהֹר
סָבִיב סָבִיב בַּמַּעְגָּל, וּלְלַמֵּד אֶת אֲבָנֶיהָ לְהִסְתַּדֵּר
בְּמִבְנֶה נוֹעָז וּמְסֻכָּן בְּקֶטַע הַסִּיּוּם.

אַחַר כָּךְ הֵן קוֹפְצוֹת לְמַטָּה עַל הָאָרֶץ
לְקוֹל תְּשׁוּאוֹת וּמִלְחָמוֹת.

וְהָעַיִן לְצִיּוֹן צוֹפִיָּה וּבוֹכִיָּה.

### Questions for Thought

1. Is Amichai's image of Jerusalem positive or negative?

2. Why are the Jews of Jerusalem "used" and "tired?"

3. Are the Jews of Jerusalem being "used?" If so, by whom?

4. In line 11, what does it mean that Jerusalem needs a "ringmaster" and not a mayor? Do you agree?

## TOURISTS

1     *Visits of condolence are what we get from them.*

2     *They squat at the Holocaust Memorial,*

3     *They put on grave faces at the Wailing Wall*

4     *And they laugh behind heavy curtains*

5     *In their hotels.*

6     *They have their pictures taken*

7     *Together with our famous dead*

8     *At Rachel's Tomb and Herzl's Tomb*

9     *And on the top of Ammunition Hill.*

10     *They weep over our sweet boys*

11     *And lust over our tough girls*

12     *And hang up their underwear*

13     *To dry quickly*

14     *In cool, blue bathrooms.*

*Once I sat on the steps by a gate at David's Tower. I placed my two heavy baskets at my side. A group of tourists was standing around their guide and I became their target marker. "You see that man with the baskets? Just right of his head there's an arch from the Roman period. Just right of his head." "But he's moving, he's moving!" I said to myself: redemption will come only if their guide tells them, "You see that arch from the Roman period? It's not important: but next to it, left and down a bit, there sits a man who's bought fruit and vegetables for his family."*

### Questions for Thought

**1. What are some of the things that tourists do which Amichai resents?**

**2. What does this reflect about the relationship between Diaspora Jews and Israelis?**

בִּקּוּרֵי אֲבֵלִים הֵם עוֹרְכִים אֶצְלֵנוּ,
יוֹשְׁבִים בְּיָד וָשֵׁם, מַרְצִינִים לְיַד הַכֹּתֶל הַמַּעֲרָבִי
וְצוֹחֲקִים מֵאֲחוֹרֵי וִילוֹנוֹת כְּבֵדִים בְּחַדְרֵי מָלוֹן,

מִצְטַלְּמִים עִם מֵתִים חֲשׁוּבִים בְּקֶבֶר רָחֵל
וּבְקֶבֶר הֶרְצֵל וּבְגִבְעַת הַתַּחְמֹשֶׁת,
בּוֹכִים עַל יְפִי גְּבוּרַת נְעָרֵינוּ
וְחוֹשְׁקִים בִּקְשִׁיחוּת נַעֲרוֹתֵינוּ
וְתוֹלִים אֶת תַּחְתּוֹנֵיהֶם
לְיִבּוּשׁ מָהִיר
בְּאַמְבַּטְיָה כְּחֻלָּה וְצוֹנֶנֶת.

פַּעַם יָשַׁבְתִּי עַל מַדְרֵגוֹת לְיַד שַׁעַר בִּמְצוּדַת דָּוִד, אֶת שְׁנֵי הַסַּלִּים הַכְּבֵדִים שַׂמְתִּי לְיָדִי. עָמְדָה שָׁם קְבוּצַת תַּיָּרִים סְבִיב הַמַּדְרִיךְ וְשִׁמַּשְׁתִּי לָהֶם נְקֻדַּת צִיּוּן. "אַתֶּם רוֹאִים אֶת הָאִישׁ הַזֶּה עִם הַסַּלִּים? קְצָת יָמִינָה מֵרֹאשׁוֹ נִמְצֵאת קֶשֶׁת מִן הַתְּקוּפָה הָרוֹמִית. קְצָת יָמִינָה מֵרֹאשׁוֹ". אֲבָל הוּא זָז, הוּא זָז! אָמַרְתִּי בְּלִבִּי: הַגְּאֻלָּה תָּבוֹא רַק אִם יַגִּידוּ לָהֶם: אַתֶּם רוֹאִים שָׁם אֶת הַקֶּשֶׁת מִן הַתְּקוּפָה הָרוֹמִית? לֹא חָשׁוּב: אֲבָל לְיָדָהּ, קְצָת שְׂמֹאלָה וּלְמַטָּה מִמֶּנָּה, יוֹשֵׁב אָדָם שֶׁקָּנָה פֵּרוֹת וִירָקוֹת לְבֵיתוֹ.

22

## Questions for Thought

1. Can a city have characteristics that actually affect its inhabitants?

2. Which image of Jerusalem do you like the most?

3. When you hear "Jerusalem," what are the first thoughts that come into your mind? Characterize your thoughts. (E.g., religious, social, imagination and reality, war and peace, etc.)

1. Each of the poems in this chapter are reprinted from: Yehuda Amichai, *Poems of Jerusalem - A Bilingual Edition*, Tel Aviv: Shocken, 1987.

# Chapter 4
## Zionism 101 - Introduction to the Critical Thinkers and Doers

In this chapter we are going to "meet" some of the key thinkers of the Zionist Movement.[1] Each answered a certain calling and had very clear views as to what he felt was the essential purpose of the Zionist Movement.

In the previous chapters we studied our relationship to Israel and Jerusalem through texts, both traditional and modern, which to a great extent emphasized that which was out of reach - the inability to fulfill the dream of returning to Israel.

With the turn of the 19th century, Zionism became not just a religious dream but a political movement, advocating the creation of a Jewish State in Palestine. This in itself is among the paradoxes of the Zionist movement. The deeply felt attachment to Eretz Yisrael which we have reviewed had remained passive for almost two thousand years. Why the sudden activity for the creation of a Jewish State?

Many will argue that new levels of anti-Semitism was the reason for the political development of the Zionist Movement in the 19th century. However using this argument begs the question of why did this response take so long to make its entrance onto the stage of Jewish history. Throughout the Middle Ages the Jewish People suffered expulsions, pogroms and blood libels. Why then did very few people turn East to Jerusalem?

What is clear, and will be emphasized by the writings of the early Zionist thinkers, is that the new freedoms for Jews in the secular society transformed this essentially religious movement into a political and nationalistic one. This new form of Zionism was a response to the challenges of liberalism, nationalism and secularism, and clearly not just to anti-Semitism. This is, to a great extent, why it occurred when it occurred.

It was in this context that Zionism changed the identity of the Jews from a traditional religious community, to a modern Nationalistic community of the Jews as a Nation. This was, and is, the fundamental revolution of the Zionist Movement.

---

[1] The selections from each Zionist thinkers writings are excerpted from: *The Zionist Idea*, ed. Arthur Hertzberg (Philadelphia, Jewish Publication Society, 1997)

Zionism as a movement, as more than an emotional expression of love for Eretz Yisrael and support of brave Jews who dared to settle in the ancestral homeland, as an organization aiming to establish a state for Jews in Palestine, was the creation of Theodore Herzl. Herzl decided to convoke an assembly of all sympathetic to his ideas. On August 19, 1897, the first World Zionist Congress was convened in Basle Switzerland. When the World Zionist Organization came into being, it was an undivided body. Soon, however, groups within it formed to seek their specific kind of Zionism. The Orthodox, for example, formed Mizrachi, a party seeking a Zionism adhering to Orthodox Judaism. Those who believed in a combination of Socialism and Zionism created their own parties. There were those "General Zionists," without a specific idealogy but not committed to any other.

In this chapter you will read about four different Zionist philosophies, with selections from the writings of their protagonists.

# Rabbi Abraham Isaac Kook

**Rav Kook was appointed to be the first Chief Rabbi of Palestine in 1921. His passionate love for Eretz Yisrael and his broad sense of tolerance for the nonreligious chalutzim endeared him to all segments of the Palestinian community. He firmly believed that the expression of modern Jewish nationalism was the beginning of an age in which the Messiah would appear, and that the labors of the secularists must be lovingly accepted for they were unwittingly serving God's purposes.**

ERETZ ISRAEL is not something apart from the soul of the Jewish people . . . Eretz Israel is part of the very essence of our nationhood; it is bound organically to its very life and inner being. Human reason, even at its most sublime, cannot begin to understand the unique holiness of Eretz Israel; it cannot stir the depths of love for the land that are dormant within our people. What Eretz Israel means to the Jew can be felt only through the Spirit of the Lord which is in our people as a whole, through the spiritual cast of the Jewish soul, which radiates its characteristic influence to every healthy emotion . . .

TO REGARD ERETZ ISRAEL as merely a tool for establishing our national unity - or even for sustaining our religion in the Diaspora by preserving its proper character and its faith, piety, and observances - is a sterile notion; it is unworthy of the holiness of Eretz Israel. A valid strengthening of Judaism in the Diaspora can come only from a deepened attachment to Eretz Israel. The hope for the return to the Holy Land - is the continuing source of the distinctive nature of Judaism. The hope for the Redemption is the force that sustains Judaism in the Diaspora; the Judaism of Eretz Israel is the very Redemption.

JEWISH ORIGINAL CREATIVITY, whether in the realm of ideas or in the arena of daily life and action, is impossible except in Eretz Israel. On the other hand, whatever the Jewish people creates in Eretz Israel assimilates the universal into characteristic and unique Jewish form, to the great benefit of the Jewish people and of the world . . .

A JEW CANNOT BE as devoted and true to his own ideas, sentiments, and imagination in the Diaspora as he can in Eretz Israel. Revelations of the Holy, of whatever degree, are relatively pure in Eretz Israel; outside it, they are mixed with dross and much impurity. However, the greater is one's yearning for and attachment to Eretz Israel, the purer his thoughts become, for they then live in the air of Eretz Israel, which sustains everyone who longs to behold the Land.

### *Questions for Thought*

1.    **What is the basis for Rav Kook's Zionism?**

2.    **According to Rav Kook's philosophy, how does Israel make ones Judaism stronger?**

3.    **Do you agree/disagree with Rav Kook's belief that Jewish original creativity is possible only in Israel? Why?**

4.    **How do <u>you</u> feel that living outside of Israel affects your Jewish ideas, sentiments, and imagination? How did Rav Kook feel about this?**

# Ahad Ha'am

**Ahad Ha'am spoke of "cultural" Zionism, the belief that Israel should become the center of Jewish life, sending Torah and Jewish learning out to the Jewish communities of the Diaspora. To him the purpose of Palestine was not to solve the problem of anti-Semitism, but to serve as a spiritual center which would revive Jewish life in the diaspora and would offer the communities spiritual strength and cultural unity. Personally not religious, he respected religion and observed many religious practices. But he insisted that Judaism was not basically a religion, that religion was just one of the phenomena of Jewish nationalism. He argued that before any attempt was made to establish a Jewish state, the Hebrew cultural survival of the Jewish People should first be secured.**

IT IS NOT ONLY THE JEWS who have come out of the ghetto; Judaism has come out, too. For the Jews the exodus from the ghetto is confined to certain countries and is due to toleration; but Judaism has come out (or is coming out) of its own accord, wherever it has come into contact with modern culture. This contact with modern culture overturns the inner defenses of Judaism, so that it can no longer remain isolated and live a life apart. The spirit of our people desires further development; it wants to absorb the basic elements of general culture which are reaching it from the outside world, to digest them and to make them a part of itself, as it has done before at various periods of its history. But the conditions of its life in exile are not suitable for such a task. In our time culture expresses itself everywhere through the form of the national spirit, and the stranger who would become part of culture must sink his individuality and become absorbed in the dominant environment. In exile, Judaism cannot, therefore, develop its individuality in its own way. When it leaves the ghetto walls, it is in danger of losing its essential being or - at very least - its national unity; it is in danger of being split up into as many kinds of Judaism, each with different character and life, as there are countries of the dispersion . . .

IT DOES NOT NEED AN INDEPENDENT STATE, but only the creation in its native land of conditions favorable to its development: a good sized settlement of Jews working without hindrance in every branch of civilization, from agriculture and handicrafts to science and literature. This Jewish settlement, which will be a gradual growth, will become in course of time the center of the nation, wherein its spirit will find pure expression and develop in all its aspects to the highest degree of perfection of which it is capable. Then, from this center, the spirit of Judaism will radiate to the great circumference, to all the communities of the Diaspora, to inspire them with new life and to preserve the overall unity of our people. When our national culture in Palestine has attained that level, we may be confident that it will produce men in the Land of Israel itself who will be able, at a favorable moment, to establish a State there - one which will be not merely a State of Jews but a really Jewish State.

## Questions for Thought

1.  **What is the basis for Ahad Ha'am's Zionism?**

2.  **How do you feel about Ahad Ha'am's position that the spirit of Judaism will emanate from Israel, as the center for Jewish life? What significance does this idea have for Jewish life in diaspora communities?**

3.  **What is the difference between a State of Jews and a Jewish State?**

# Theodore Herzl

**Theodore Herzl was shocked by the unjust treatment of a French Jewish soldier, Captain Alfred Dreyfus, and decided that Jews could be safe only if they had a state of their own. His book, *The Jewish State*, attracted world attention. His ideas seemed fantastic and impractical, and aroused the opposition of Jews from many different beliefs. Despite the opposition, Herzl almost singlehandedly organized the First Zionist Congress, the first official gathering of world Jewish leaders. Through the Congress and the World Zionist Organization, Herzl established the organizations which would eventually create the State of Israel.**

ANTI-SEMITISM IS A HIGHLY COMPLEX MOVEMENT, which I think I understand. I approach this movement as a Jew, yet without fear or hatred. I believe that I can see it in the elements of cruel sport, of common commercial rivalry, of inherited prejudice, of religious intolerance - but also of a supposed need for self-defense. I consider the Jewish question neither a social nor a religious one, even though it sometimes takes these and other forms. It is a national question, and to solve it we must first of all establish it as an international political problem to be discussed and settled by the civilized nations of the world in council.

We are a people - *one* people.

WE HAVE SINCERELY TRIED everywhere to merge with the national communities in which we live, seeking only to preserve the faith of our fathers. It is not permitted us. In vain are we loyal patriots, sometimes superloyal; in vain do we make the same sacrifices of life and property as our fellow citizens; in vain do we strive to enhance the fame of our native lands in the arts and sciences, or her wealth by trade and commerce. In our native lands where we have lived for centuries we are still decried as aliens, often by men whose ancestors had not yet come at a time when Jewish sighs had long been heard in the country . . . In the world as it now is and will probably remain, for an indefinite period, might takes precedence over right. It is without avail, therefore, for us to be loyal patriots . . . If we were left in peace . . .

But I think we shall not be left in peace.

OPPRESSION AND PERSECUTION cannot exterminate us. No nation on earth has endured such struggles and sufferings as we have . . . Wherever we remain politically secure for any length of time, we assimilate. I think this is not praiseworthy.

The whole plan is essentially quite simple, as it must necessarily be if it is to be comprehensible to all.

Let sovereignty be granted us over a portion of the globe adequate to meet our rightful traditional requirements; we will attend to the rest . . .

WE MUST NOT VISUALIZE the exodus of the Jews as a sudden one. It will be gradual, proceeding over a period of decades. The poorest will go first and cultivate the soil. They will construct roads, bridges, railways, and telegraph installations, regulate rivers, and provide themselves with homesteads, all according to predetermined plans. Their labor will create trade, trade will create markets, and markets will attract new settlers - for every man will go voluntarily, at his own expense and his own risk. The labor invested in the soil will enhance its value. The Jews will soon perceive that a new and permanent frontier has been opened up for that spirit of enterprise which has heretofore brought them only hatred and obloquy . . .

### _Questions for Thought_

1.  **What is the basis of Herzl's Zionism?**
2.  **According to Herzl, the solution to Jewish sovereignty relies upon granting the Jewish people a "portion of the globe." Why must this be in Israel?**
3.  **What do you like about Herzl's plan? What disturbs you?**

# A.D. Gordon

Aaron David Gordon settled in Palestine in 1904 at the age of fifty and preached a "religion of labor." Labor Zionism spoke of the return to nature as the basis of the return to Zion. To Gordon, the Jewish people could be reborn through the reeducation and moral conduct of the Jewish individual and through love of the soil, and of work. He himself served as an exemplar through his personal life and work. He felt that labor must become the chief ideal of the Jewish people, of the educated and uneducated alike. In his opinion there was no conflict between intellectual growth and the life of nature through work.

THE JEWISH PEOPLE has been completely cut off from nature and imprisoned within city walls these two thousand years. We have become accustomed to every form of life, except to a life of labor - of labor done at our own behest and for its own sake. It will require the greatest effort of will for such a people to become normal again. We lack the principal ingredient for national life. We lack the habit of labor - not labor performed out of external compulsion, but labor to which one is attached in a natural and organic way. This kind of labor binds a people to its soil and to its national culture, which in turn is an outgrowth of the people's soil and the people's labor.

NOW IT IS TRUE that every people has many individuals who shun physical labor and try to live off the work of others. But a normal people is like a living organism which performs its various functions naturally, and labor is one of its basic and organic functions. A normal people invariably contains a large majority of individuals for whom labor is second nature. But we Jews are different. We have developed an attitude of looking down on manual labor, so that even those who are engaged in it work out of mere compulsion and always with the hope of eventually escaping to "a better life." We must not deceive ourselves in this regard, nor shut our eyes to our grave deficiencies, not merely as individuals but as a people. The well-known Talmudic saying that when the Jews do God's will their labor is done for them by others, is characteristic of our attitude. This saying is significant. It demonstrates how far this attitude has become an instinctive feeling within us, a second nature.

...WE ARE A PEOPLE WITHOUT A COUNTRY, without a living national language, without a living culture - but that, at least, we know and it pains us, even if only vaguely, and we seek ways and means of doing what needs must be done. But we seem to think that if we have no labor it does not matter - let Ivan, or John, or Mustapha do the work, while we busy ourselves with producing a culture, with creating national values, and with enthroning absolute justice in the world.

WHAT ARE WE SEEKING IN PALESTINE? Is it not that which we can never find elsewhere - the fresh milk of a healthy people's culture? What we are come to create at present is not the culture of the academy, before we have anything else, but a culture of life, of which the culture of the academy is one element. We seek to create a vital culture out of which the cream of higher culture can easily be evolved. We intend to create creeds and ideologies, art and poetry, and ethics and religion, all growing out of a healthy life and intimately related to it; we shall therefore have created healthy human relationships and living links that bind the present to the past. What we seek to create here is life - our own life - in our own spirit and in our own way. Let me put it more bluntly. In Palestine we must do with our own hands all the things that make up the sum total of life. We must ourselves do all the work, from the least strenuous, cleanest, and most sophisticated, to the dirtiest and most difficult. In our own way, we must feel what a worker feels and think what a worker thinks - then, and only then, shall we have a culture of our own . . .

WHAT WE NEED ARE ZEALOTS OF LABOR - zealots in the finest sense of the word. Any man who devotes his life to this ideal will not need to be told how difficult it is, but he will also know that it is of immense importance.

## Questions for Thought

1.    What is the focus of A.D. Gordon's Zionism?
2.    What do you see as the strengths and weaknesses of Gordon's position?

## Questions for Thought

1. List reasons why you feel it took so long for there to be an active movement to create a Jewish State.

2. Which of the early Zionist thinkers do you agree with most and why?

3. What are the similarities and differences between each of the Zionist thinkers?

4. Keeping in mind what you have read from each of these Zionist thinkers, write a paragraph defining your own Zionism.

   _____

   _____

   _____

   _____

   _____

   _____

   _____

   _____

5. Explain your answer to each of the following questions:

   a) Can one be Jewish and not a Zionist?
   b) Can one be a Zionist and not Jewish?
   c) Can one be an Israeli and not be a Zionist?

## Activity

Imagine that an election is being held for President of the "Zionist Thinkers Association." Choose one of the four Zionist thinkers discussed in this chapter, create a slogan, and develop his major campaign points.

## An Look at Hatikvah: Israel's National Anthem[1]

Hatikvah, the national anthem of the State of Israel, was written by Naphtali Imber in 1878. Several years later Samuel Cohen set the poem to a well-known melodic type which was common throughout Europe.

In 1898 and again in 1900 there were competitions for a Zionist anthem. On both occasions, no anthem was selected because of the poor quality of the songs suggested. At the fifth Zionist Congress in 1901 one of the sessions concluded with the singing of Imber's poem, entitled *Tikvateinu* at that time. Despite its rapid ascent as the anthem of the Zionist Movement, it was not until the eighteenth Zionist Congress in 1933 that it was formally adopted. Under the British Mandate, Hatikvah was the unofficial anthem of Jewish Palestine.

Hatikvah, the national anthem of the State of Israel, contains several attributes that express the uniqueness of Jewish life:

1) It was written before Israel became an independent state.
2) It was written in Hebrew, many years before Hebrew became the language of the Jewish State. Indeed, at the time it was penned, Hebrew was used only as a language of prayer and traditional Jewish study.
3) It was written outside of the future state, in Europe. The anthem hints of this when it states, "With eyes turned eastward looking towards Zion

In general, other nations who have attained independence have done so while present in their own land and while speaking a living language. Jews had to migrate from abroad to their land, acquire their language, and, after that, to fight for independence.

> **HATIKVAH**
> *As long as in the heart*
> *The Jewish spirit yearns*
> *With eyes turned eastward*
> *Looking towards Zion, then our hope,*
> *The hope of two thousand years,*
> *Is not lost;*
> *To be a free nation in our land,*
> *The land of Zion and Jerusalem*

---

[1] The material in this section was adapted from *Hatikvah: Learning Together*, a publication of the American Zionist Youth Foundation and the Education and Culture Department.

Hatikvah comprises two parts; the second segment describes a hope, and the first section provides conditions for the fulfillment of this hope.

## A Religious or Secular Poem?

The dream of a return to Zion is integral to the Jewish religion. The words of Hatikvah represent the transformation of religious language to the language of modern nationalism. Phrases such as "the Jewish spirit yearns" and "with eyes turned eastward looking towards Zion" can be understood in religious terms, but are secular. In fact, Hatikvah is a surprisingly secular poem. For example, God is not mentioned. However, Hatikvah is not anti-religious. It describes religious feelings in secular language. It defines the religious concept of redemption as nationalist hope. It represents the Zionist link between religious desire and modern, nationalistic aspirations.

## Spiritual Power

It is interesting that "to be a free nation in our land"does not hinge on political or economic power, but rather, on spiritual power -- on what is in our hearts and minds. This emphasis on internal commitment to the land is very typical of Jewish thought.

## Individual Hope or National Aspiration

Note the relationship between the singular and the plural. Hatikvah expresses the idea of a private hope transformed into a national aspiration - to transform an individual hope into "our hope." The nation, in this poem, is dependent on the individual.

## The Importance of East

An important aspect of Hatikvah is its emphasis on the east. The Hebrew word *kedem* means east. The word *kadima* means eastward, but it also means moving forward. Our ancestors attached special, positive meaning to the direction from which the sun rose. The east, in Jewish thought, symbolizes both the future and the hope.

## Questions for Thought

1. How do you feel when you sing the Hatikvah? Has there been a particular time or event when you sang it that was particularly meaningful?

2. If Hatikvah is, as its title indicates, about hope, is its tone optimistic or pessimistic? What specific hope does Hatikvah describe? Has the hope of the song been fulfilled?

3. Is the poem's vision for the future a religious one?

4. How do you understand the phrase "As long as in the heart the Jewish spirit yearns." Can you give at least one example of an instance when you felt this type of yearning?

5. Hatikvah was written more than one century ago. Is the existence of the State of Israel still conditional? On what does it depend?

   Do you feel that diaspora Jewry depends upon Israel as a homeland or as a source of Jewish identification?

6. Write your own conditional sentence that expresses your understanding of the relationship between Israel and world Jewry. The sentence should begin with the phrase -

   "As long as_____

# THE JEWISH TOWN

# TEL-AVIV

KEREN HAYESOD

JERUSALEM

1932

# Chapter 5
## Between Tel Aviv and New York: Two Promised Lands

Both New York and Jerusalem have been, and continue to be, ports of call for Jewish immigrants.

In the writings which follow we will see a remarkable resemblance in the image of both these promised lands.

A further paradox of the Zionist Revolution is that most Jews who are able to choose, choose not to live in Israel, but yet choose aspects of the Jewish Homeland as identifying features of their community.

Among the challenges that we will continue to face is further developing a meaningful dialogue between Israel and Diaspora Jews. At the close of the 20th century, many in Israel are more accepting of the fact that we will continue to be disparate communities, and are grappling with ways of making our relationship more meaningful.

Does this mean that we must strive to be more similar? Many of the following passages may imply this, but as Hillel Halkin recently observed in an update to his book "Letter to an American Friend" - *"You're more comfortable with us when we're more like you - and we mean less to you when we are."*

## The American Dream

In the single generation between 1881 and 1914, the Jewish population in America increased from 250,000 to 3 million. The need of these Jews, mainly from Eastern Europe, was first and foremost survival from ongoing persecution and violence.

In these years a growing number of publications glorified the "American Dream," and illustrated it as a continent whose streets were paved with gold. In a story by I.N Dick, a popular Yiddish novelist of Vilna, America was identified as the biblical land of Ophir, from which Hiram of Tyre had fetched the gold for the building of King Solomon's Temple. Other tales by Dick had various Jewish characters find their fortune and happy endings in this new promised land.

Sholom Aleichem, perhaps the most popular Yiddish writer of the turn of the century, presented America as a land of marvels where people did not walk - they ran. They write fast, talk fast and speed from place to place under the ground. It is the only land of true liberty and equality. He suggested that a person ought to wash his hands - as a pious Jew does before saying his prayers - before uttering the sacred name of 'America,' God's finest handiwork.

Through these ideas Sholom Aleichem enabled and encouraged Jews to view themselves differently. In a sense, the promise of this Land afforded the Jew the chance of creating for him or herself a new identity.

It is clear that the golden dreams of America as a modern Garden of Eden dissipated when the Jewish immigrants faced economic hardships and the need to adjust to an alien environment. Nonetheless, the dominant theme which occurs in all the reports which immigrants sent back to the old country was that of optimism and that the struggle, hard as it was, would end successfully.

What was to become of the Jews' identity in this New World? "The Melting Pot" was the title given by novelist Israel Zangwill to his much publicized drama of 1908 (5 years after the Kishinev Pogrom of 1903)[1] in which he advocated assimilation and

---

[1] On April 6-7, 1903, a pogrom in Kishinev, Russia resulted in the destruction of 1300 Jewish homes and businesses and 2000 Jews being left homeless. The basis of the pogrom was a false story of the murder of a Russian youth at the hands of the Jews for ritual purposes. Agents of the Ministry of Interior

intermarriage for the Jews of the New World. For the Jews in America (as opposed to Jews who remained in Europe) Zangwill was prepared to throw away the entire heritage of the past. He was confident that the new product which would emerge, the new man and the new culture, would be far better than the old. "The sooner the new immigrants would give up their cultural characteristics and melt into the undifferentiated mass, the sooner anti-Semitism would disappear."[2]

While the cries of the victims of the Kishinev Pogrom of 1903 were still echoing throughout the Jewish world, Zangwill projected as the hero of his drama a young survivor of this massacre and as the heroine, the daughter of the pogrom leader. He devised a plot whereby both meet in a New York settlement house and fall in love with each other. Ingrained prejudices that would have kept them apart abroad, lose their virulence and relevance in the new country. Here they experience the cleansing effect of America, the great crucible that dissolves all race differences and vendettas.

Let us compare this advocacy of Zangwill's "New Jew" to the great Hebrew poet Chaim Nachman Bialik's Jew as portrayed in the "City of Slaughter," also written shortly after the Kishinev pogrom of 1903. Here, neither God nor the Russian mobs are blamed, but Bialik severely berates the Jews for their passivity and cowardice and their continued adherence to traditional Jewish beliefs. Later in this controversial piece, Bialik demands self redemption of the Jews NOT in the exile, but in Israel.

> *The earth is as it was, the sun still shines.*
> *It is a day like any other day.*
> *Descend then, to the cellars of the town,*
> *There where the virginal daughters of thy folk were fouled,*
> *Where seven heathen flung a woman down . . .*
> *Crouched husbands, bridegrooms, brothers, peering from the cracks,*
> *Watching the sacred bodies struggling underneath*
> *The bestial breath,*
> *Stifled in filth, and swallowing their blood!*
> *Watching from the darkness and its mesh . . .*
> *Crushed in their shame, they saw it all;*

and high ranking local officials were apparently involved in the preparation of the pogrom. This marked the beginning of a period of violent anti-Semitism in Russia and resulted in a large emigration of Jews to America, and a smaller number of emigrants to Palestine in the Second Aliyah.

[2]Henry Feingold, *Zion in America* (Twayne Publishers, Inc., 1974, 1981) p. 147.

*They did not stir nor move . . .*
*Perhaps, perhaps, each watcher had it in his heart to pray:*
*A miracle, O Lord, - and spare my skin this day!*
*Those who survived this foulness, who from their blood awoke,*
*Beheld their life polluted, the light of their world gone out -*
*How did their menfolk bear it, how did they bear this yoke?*
*They crawled forth from their holes, they fled to the house of the Lord,*
*They offered thanks to Him, the sweet benedictory word . . .*
*The matter ends; and nothing more.*
*And all is as it was before.*

Four years after Zangwill's play was first produced, Mary Antin's autobiography, 'The Promised Land,' was published. Its first sentence read:

*"I was born, I have lived, and I have been made over . . . "*

What Mary Antin implied was:
I was born a Jewess. I lived the life of a Jewess in Russia. I came to America and I have been made over as an American. She continues her plea to **forget.** In her book, America was The Promised Land where the wandering Jew could become the pure American.

Born to a New York Sephardi family, Emma Lazarus started writing in her early teens. She was heavily influenced by Ralph Waldo Emerson, and she published several influential books of poetry. Emma Lazarus took a deep interest in Jewish affairs, speaking out against anti-Semitism in a number of her works. Yet, after her death, her sister prohibited the inclusion of "anything Jewish" in collected editions of her work. In 1883 Lazarus entered a poetry contest organized to raise money to build a pedestal for the Statue of Liberty. Her prize-winning poem, written in honor of Russian Jews, is inscribed on the base of the statue.

*Here at our sea-washed, sunset gates shall stand a mighty woman with a torch,*
*Whose flame is the imprisoned lighting, and her name*
*Mother of exiles, from her beacon hand glows world-wide welcome;*
*Her mild eyes command the air-bridged harbor that twin cities frame,*
*"Keep ancient lands, your storied pomp!"*
*Cries she with silent lips. "Give me your tired your poor, Your huddled masses*
*Yearning to breath free, the wretched refuse of your teaming shore,*
*Send these, the homeless, tempest-fast to me, I lift my lamp beside the golden door!"*

What could be more welcoming to the Jews who filled almost every category of Lazarus's "calling." The "mighty woman" is waiting to welcome her 'tired:' tired of the exile and those wanting a new tomorrow.

## The New Jew

As we have seen, the early 1880's witnessed mass migrations of Jews, which dramatically changed the character and geographic location of the Jewish communities of the world. The vast majority fled west, but approximately 25,000 went to Palestine. What is the calling that these people heard? They too wished to create a New Reality with a New Jew. Some saw themselves as forerunners of a community that would provide inspiration to Jews all over the world, and provide refuge in time of need. Many continued the tradition of settlement in the 'Holy Land,' which required them to live in the four holy cities (Tiberias, Safed, Hebron and Jerusalem) and by so doing, hasten the coming of the Messiah through their piety. Economic hardships very much dampened these messianic yearnings, however, and the "Second Aliyah," to a great extent introduced the new Jew to the stage of Jewish History. These settlers became very critical of their predecessors, yet both shared the opinion that the major task of Zionism was the settlement of Jews on the land in Palestine. Their focus was that the return to the Land of Israel implied a return to the land. This led to the belief in the need to adjust the mentality of the Jew, who for many hundreds of years had been forbidden to own land and had been cut off from productive occupations by legislative and other means.

It is important to relate to these motivations, in order to understand the difference between those Jews who went West and those who went to Palestine. Immigrants to the United States arrived hoping to start a new life in the new world. This encouraged the replacement of the "old" by the "new." In Palestine there was not the "new culture" to replace the old. Here one had to be *invented.* Here the call was for the creation of a new Jewish People and a new Jew in the Land of Israel.

Whereas many of the assimilationists advocated giving up Jewish culture, the Zionists sought a return to the "purity" and "authenticity" of the existence of the Hebrew nation in its land. What both the assimilationists and the Zionists shared, however, was the acceptance of the negative Jewish stereotypes promulgated by non-Jews, and adopted by them to their own purpose.

In Palestine, the new Jew had the Hebrew worker sitting on a wooden box, eating Arabic bread dipped in olive oil. This expressed simultaneously three new phenomena; he is a worker, he is a "true son of the land" and he is not eating in a "Jewish" way (he is not at a table and he has not fulfilled the obligation to wash his hands and make a blessing).

**Illustration of the "New Jew" from a 1937 publication of *Keren Kayemet L'Yisrael*.**

Hence, our return to Palestine was a return to our "Hebrew" roots, the nomadic, productive Jew. The meaning of this "auto-emancipation" was the conversion of the Jews from being an object of history to being a subject of history. The Jews were creating a living national body with independent national self-consciousness, with shared goals and programmes for achieving them.

The ongoing journeys to the "promised Lands" of New York and Tel Aviv created fascinating use of concepts and language common to both groups of immigrants. They will no doubt continue to deeply affect our very understanding of Jewish Identity and community in the years to come.

Demoralized, frustrated, and embittered after the 1973 Yom Kippur War, serving two months a year in the IDF reserve, Hillel Halkin was only two years into his aliyah. "I was angry at American Jews, who, even if they thought they cared about Israel, didn't very much. And I needed to justify to myself why I was in Israel." The result: *Letters to an American Jewish Friend*, written to a fictional composite. *Letters* made waves . . . What follows reveals Israel and Halkin, still irrevocably bound (21 years later), but Halkin and American Jews needing to forgive each other for shattered myths.

═══════════

*Zichron Ya'akov*
*December 15, 1997*

*Dear A--,*

*It has been a long while, hasn't it? 20 years . . . ! And now you write that you are coming on a visit . . .*

*It will be good to see you. And I promise, there will be no arguments like the ones 20 years ago . . . and not a word from me about why Israel is the only place for a Jew like you to live.*

*Not that I've changed my mind. But I couldn't write those letters today . . .*

*They were written, those letters, on a fine edge of anger and hope. It's been a long time since I've felt either toward you.*

*Why be angry at you for living your life comfortably where it was given you, surrounded by everything to which you are accustomed? Why hope that a mere intellectual analysis could persuade you to give up that life . . . ?*

*Assimilation? Intermarriage? A statistically dwindling American Jewish community? It was pointless to wave such threats at you. Unlike hunger or persecution, you can live with them. Jews in America-a few more, a few less-there will always be; with a bit of luck, some of your grandchildren may be among them. And would you worry less if you lived in Israel? Would it be better to fear losing a child to the Hezbollah in Lebanon, or even to an academic career in New York, than to a non-Jewish marriage in Los Angeles?*

*You have won, my friend. The chances of my children ending up in America along with hundreds of thousands of other ex-Israelis are far greater than those of yours ending up in Israel . . .*

*For years you've been hearing and reading about an Israel that is "Americanized," that is "post-Zionist," that has become like everywhere else. And while half of you has always wanted this for us ("How can you live* in a place where you can't even get a decent hamburger?" I remember you asking me on your last visit), the other half fears finding out that it is true.

And it is true. We not only have your hamburger now, we have all the rest of it too, from shopping malls to suburban sprawl. You'll feel far more at home here today-and less convinced than ever that there is any reason to make it your home, since you don't lack shopping and suburbs in America.

I suppose this has always been the paradox of American Jewish attitudes toward Israel. You're more comfortable with us when we're more like you-and we mean less to you when we are.

And we will go on becoming more like you, call it Americanization, or globalization, or whatever you like . . .

The idea that Israel was or could be a substitute religion for American Jews never had any rational basis to begin with. No community can live vicariously for long through an identification with another community. If you are going to go on living as Jews in America, you will have to look to yourselves for the ways and reasons to do so. We could not be of much help to you even if we wanted to be.

True, we have too much in common to drift totally apart. Some contacts may even grow as we converge. Jews with specific interests and inclinations in America may forge closer ties with similarly inclined Jews in Israel. But Israel as a cause will cease to exist for you, just as the Diaspora as a mission has ceased to exist for us.

We'll get over it. No one likes being demoted. But although it was flattering to be the center of your world for a while, being your inspiration was too tall an order for us. You wanted us to be your model Jews. There was no way we could have lived up to that . . .

Well, we in Israel have had the chance and have not done so marvelously well-not because of any tragic mistake that we have committed, but because our Jewish superiority was a myth to begin with, one perpetuable only in exile, where we could let the gentiles make a mess of things and mock them for it. It's hard for you to forgive us for this . . .

For all its disappointments, Israel is who we are, uncamouflaged and unadorned. Whatever it has or has not accomplished, whatever it will or will not accomplish in the future, is exactly what we Jews are capable of when left to ourselves, with only our own resources to draw on and no goyim to blame or learn better manners from.

To find out at last who we really are! I wouldn't have wanted to miss it for the world.

See you soon,

Hillel

**Excerpted from *Moment Magazine*, April 1998 issue, with the author's permission.**

## Exercises

**1. Put yourself in the place of a Russian Jew soon after the Kishinev pogrom of 1903. You know that you must leave Russia, but should you emigrate to North America or Palestine? List the pros and cons of each location.**

<u>North America - Pro</u>                                    <u>Palestine - Pro</u>

<u>North America - Con</u>                                    <u>Palestine - Con</u>

**2. Take the position of Hillel Halkin's American friend and write a letter in return with your reactions to his points.**

_____

_____

_____

_____

_____

_____

_____

_____

# Chapter 6
## Israel's Declaration of Independence

Of all the texts that give a truly insightful picture as to what kind of country Israel was going to be, the Declaration of Independence is a remarkable expression of that dream.

This historic moment, the formal declaration of Israel's statehood, was fraught with meaning. But which meaning? Rabbi Jonathan Sacks, in <u>One People? Tradition, Modernity and Jewish Unity</u>, observes that, "Jews use the same words but mean profoundly different things by them." He goes on to mention the composition of this very document.

In a Religious context, the people of Israel were returning to their Promised Land, bringing the period of exile to an end. This was to be seen as "The beginning of the process of the redemption," where the Hand of God was again manifest in Jewish history. Other groups had no interest in these kinds of religious references and understood the Zionist enterprise to a great extent, as an escape from the confines of religious practice. Hence religious groups were insistent that the Declaration should contain clear references to God, whereas secularists were equally insistent on its absence. The line which states "Placing our trust in the Rock of Israel . . . " may have been the compromise. For the religious, Rock of Israel (*Tsur Yisrael*) was a clear reference to God, for the secular it represented the Jewish People and their impregnable will to be a nation with the nations of the world.

How these and numerous other conflicting visions were to be resolved can be read "between the lines." Every word and expression has various nuances, and the following "Talmudic-like" text affords an opportunity to grapple with these echoes of eternity.

## *Exercise*

**Before reading this chapter, list a number of different points that you would include if you were writing a Declaration of Independence for a new Jewish State.**

- _____
- _____
- _____
- _____
- _____

- _____
- _____
- _____
- _____
- _____

# The Declaration of the Establishment of the State of Israel

(On 5 Iyar 5708 (May 14, 1948), on the day in which the British Mandate over Palestine expired, the Jewish People's Council gathered at the Tel Aviv Museum, and approved the following proclamation, declaring the establishment of the State of Israel.)

*ERETZ ISRAEL was the birthplace of the Jewish people.[1] Here their spiritual, religious, and political identity was shaped. Here they first attained to statehood, created cultural values of national and universal significance, and gave to the world the eternal Book of Books.[2]*

*After being forcibly exiled from their land, the people kept faith with it[3] throughout their Dispersion and never ceased to pray and hope for their return to it and for the restoration in it of their political freedom.[4]*

---

1

**Eretz Israel was the birthplace of the Jewish people** (Martin Buber) It is impossible to appreciate the real meaning of 'Zion' so long as one regards it as simply one of many other national concepts. We speak of a 'national concept' when a people makes its unity, spiritual coherence, historical character, traditions, origins and evolution, destiny and vocation the objects of its conscious life and the motive power behind its actions. In this sense the Zion concept of the Jewish people can be called a national concept. But its essential quality lies precisely in that which differentiates it from all other national concepts.

It is significant that this national concept was named after a place and not, like the others, after a people, which indicates that it is not so much a question of a particular people as such but of its association with a particular land, its native land.

2

**Here they first attained to statehood . . . and gave to the world the eternal Book of Books** (Ahad Ha'am) Neither the Jewish outlook nor the Jewish faith are the original cause, the prime mover [for Zionism]; but rather the Jewish feeling, an instinctive feeling, which it is impossible to define in words.

3

**The people kept faith with it** (Shlomo Goren) Zionism has in effect existed since the time of Abraham. The connecting link between the people was the Torah and their attachment to the land of Israel. The entire Jewish people prayed facing Jerusalem. But not all were religious. Zionism revived and renewed this latent tie with Eretz Israel.

4

**The people kept their faith with it throughout their Dispersion...and for the restoration in it of their political freedom** (J. Goren) Hallucinatory gratifications kept the wish alive and focused...manifested by the Jewish ability to experience major but remote historical events as 'only yesterday' or even as present sources of joy or distress . . .until the Jews were able to opt for the real Zion, instead of having to be content with the dream of Zion as their only form of wish fulfillment.

50

*Impelled by this historic and traditional attachment, Jews strove in every successive generation to reestablish themselves in their ancient homeland. In recent decades they returned in their masses.[5] Pioneers, ma'apilim* [immigrants coming to Israel in defiance of restrictive legislation], *and defenders, they made deserts bloom, revived the Hebrew language, built villages and towns and created a thriving community, controlling its own economy and culture, loving peace by knowing how to defend itself, bringing the blessings of progress to all the country's inhabitants, and aspiring toward independent nationhood.[6]*

*In 5657 (1897), at the summons of the spiritual father of the Jewish State, Theodor Herzl[7], the First Zionist Congress convened and proclaimed the right of the Jewish people to national rebirth in its own country.*

*This right was recognized in the Balfour Declaration of the 2nd of November, 1917, and reaffirmed in the Mandate of the League of Nations which, in particular, gave international sanction to the historic connection of the Jewish people the status of a fully privileged member of the community of nations.*

*The catastrophe which recently befell the Jewish people-the massacre of millions of jews in Europe-was another clear demonstration of the urgency of solving the problem of its homelessness by reestablishing in Eretz Israel the Jewish State, which would open the gates of the homeland wide to every Jew and confer upon the Jewish people the status of a fully privileged member of the community of nations.*

---

[5]

**In recent decades they returned in their masses** (Rav Kook) Eretz Israel's manifestly providential revival was designed to fortify Israel's material foundations...whose enhancement will release the Jewish people's divine spirituality, so that the entire Torah will be restored to its former strength, to become a light unto the world.

[6]

**Pioneers, ma'apilim . . . aspiring towards independent nationhood** (Y. Bin-Nun) The Zionist process did not end with the establishment of the State of Israel. On the contrary, it only then began to operate with powerful state tools to achieve the goals of aliyah, settlement, the blossoming of the desert, and the development of science and of Torah.

[7]

**At the summons of the spiritual father of the Jewish State, Theodor Herzl** (Georges Friedman) There is no Jewish nation. There is an Israeli nation. The state that came into existence as a result of Herzl's prophecies is not a 'Jewish State.' The Israeli State is creating an imperious national community that is conscious of itself but does not include in the consciousness belonging to the 'Jewish People.'

*Survivors of the Nazi Holocaust in Europe, as well as Jews from other parts of the world, continued to migrate to Eretz-Israel, undaunted by difficulties, restrictions and dangers, and never ceased to assert their right to a life of dignity, freedom and honest toil in their national homeland.*[8]

*In the Second World War, the Jewish community of this country contributed its full share to the struggle of the freedom-and peace-loving nations against the force of Nazi wickedness and, by the blood of its soldiers and its war effort, gained the right to be reckoned among the peoples who founded the United Nations.*

*On the 29th of November, 1947, the United Nations General Assembly passed a resolution calling for the establishment of a Jewish State in Eretz-Israel; the General Assembly required the inhabitants of Eretz-Israel to take such steps as were necessary on their part for the implementation of that resolution.*[9] *This recognition by the United Nations of the right of the Jewish people to establish their State is irrevocable.*

*This right is the natural right of the Jewish people to be masters of their own fate, like all other nations, in their own sovereign State.*[10]

*ACCORDINGLY WE, MEMBERS OF THE PEOPLE'S COUNCIL, REPRESENTATIVES OF THE JEWISH COMMUNITY OF ERETZ-ISRAEL AND OF THE ZIONIST MOVEMENT, ARE HERE ASSEMBLED ON THE DAY OF THE TERMINATION OF THE BRITISH*

---

8

**Survivors of the Nazi Holocaust in Europe . . . national homeland** (Harold Fisch) The implication [meant through] the capture and trial of [Nazi Official] Eichmann [in the 1960s], Israel was somehow making good the failure of those who died without resisting. [This was a] demonstration of state power...in the states handling of the prosecution much was made, both implicitly and explicitly, of the analogy between the Nazi plan to exterminate the Jewish people and the Pan-Arab design to liquidate the State of Israel...as though to indicate that Jewish would never again be led helplessly to the slaughter...

9

**On the 29th of November...to take such steps as were necessary on their part for the implementation of that resolution.** (Walid Khalidi) "The [UNGA resolution of 29th November 1947] meant, in effect, the establishment of a Zionist state on Palestinian soil irrespective of the wishes of the overwhelming majority of its inhabitants and was taken by the Zionist leadership as a green light to launch their long contemplated [conquest].

10

**This recognition by the United Nations of the right...like all other nations, in their own sovereign State** (J. Goren) Jewish history was perceived as beleaguered by inferiorities, defects and fatal flaws . . . [But] Zionism was going to change all that. To the scattered it offered an ingathering; to the stateless, a state; to the helpless, mastery; to the passive, activity. Put more blatantly, to the inferior Jews, it promised a new generation of freedom which eventually culminated in the sabra 'superman.'

*MANDATE OVER ERETZ-ISRAEL AND, BY VIRTUE OF OUR NATURAL AND HISTORIC RIGHT AND ON THE STRENGTH OF THE RESOLUTION OF THE UNITED NATIONS GENERAL ASSEMBLY, HEREBY DECLARE THE ESTABLISHMENT OF A JEWISH STATE IN ERETZ-ISRAEL, TO BE KNOWN AS THE STATE OF ISRAEL.*

*WE DECLARE that, with effect of the moment of the termination of the Mandate, being tonight, the eve of Sabbath, the 6th Iyar, 5708 (15th May, 1948), until the establishment of the elected regular authorities of the State in accordance with the Constitution which shall be adopted by the Elected Constituent Assembly not later than the 1st October, 1948, the People's Council shall act as a Provisional Council of State, and its executive organ, the People's Administration, shall be the Provisional Government of the Jewish State, to be called "Israel."*

*THE STATE OF ISRAEL will be open for Jewish Immigration and for the Ingathering of the Exiles;[11] it will foster the development of the country for the benefit of all inhabitants; it will be based on freedom, justice, and peace as envisaged by the prophets of Israel; it will ensure complete equality of social and political rights to all its inhabitants irrespective of religion, race, or sex;[12] it will guarantee freedom of religion,[13] conscience, language, education, and culture;[14] it will be faithful to the principles of the Charter of the United Nations.*

---

[11]

**The State of Israel will be open for Jewish Immigration and for the Ingathering of the Exiles** (Arthur Koestler) Now the mission of the wandering Jew is completed, he must discard the knapsack and cease to be an accomplice in his own destruction.

[12]

**It will ensure complete equality...irrespective of religion, race or sex** (Muki Tsur) One of the main achievements of Zionism is the absolute legitimization of secular life. The return of the Jew as a full-fledged player on the state of national history has dictated a pluralism in which all forms of Jewish life, secular and religious, can find expression.

[13]

**It will guarantee freedom of religion** (Yehuda Bauer) Halacha is a matter of voluntary observance. The spectacle of a secular Knesset enacting religious laws is unseemly. There is not one "Torat Israel" – but many "Torot Israel" – and this must be recognized. (Y. Burg) Jewish secularism is possible, and, according to the experience of history, can last for a maximum of one or two generations.

[14]

**The State of Israel will be open . . . . freedom of religion, conscience, language, education and culture** (Shlomo Goren) The state is a formal framework of government. It is not the kingdom of Israel, embodying holiness and majesty. But, aside from foreign, defense, economic and political matters, it is a framework which must carry out the tasks of the prophetic vision, namely:
    1. The liberation of the land; to prepare the land to receive the Jewish people.

*THE STATE OF ISRAEL is prepared to cooperate with the agencies of the United Nations in implementing the resolution of the General Assembly of the 29th November 1947, and will take steps to bring about the economic union of the whole of Eretz-Israel.[15]*

*WE APPEAL to the United Nations to assist the Jewish people in the building-up of its State and to receive the State of Israel into the community of nations.*

*WE APPEAL - in the very midst of the onslaught launched against us now for months - to the Arab inhabitants of the State of Israel to preserve peace and participate in the upbuilding of the State on the basis of full and equal citizenship and due representation in all its provisional and permanent institutions.[16]*

*WE EXTEND out hand to all neighboring states and their peoples in an offer of peace and good neighborliness, and appeal to them to establish bonds of cooperation and mutual help with the sovereign Jewish people settled in its own land. The State of Israel is prepared to do its share in common effort for the advancement of the entire Middle East.*

---

2. The ingathering of the exiles; to carry out the messianic task of ingathering the exiles.
3. To transform Eretz Israel into the source of the revival of Jewish culture, into a workshop of Jewish creativity.
This is the function of the state vis-a-vis the entire Jewish people.

15

**and will take steps to bring about the economic union of the whole of Eretz-Israel** (Tzvi Bisk) The central Zionist challenge of our day is the transformation of Israel into the world's most developed and sophisticated society and economy, the world's first space age society . . .If we set the space age society as our aim, we will be able to exploit Jewish brainpower to the same if not greater extent that we have exploited Jewish financial power . . .We will create the tools which will allow Diaspora Jewry to contribute their abilities to the building of Israel. Israel as a space age society must be an all-Jewish challenge. As the socio-ethical laboratory for the entire Jewish people, Israel would be the central tool for Jewish survival in fact and not only in slogan.

16

**We appeal - in the very midst of the onslaught...in all its provisional and permanent institutions** (Rufus Learsi) The restoration of the Jewish state was not destined to be the result of a mere decree...most imminent, were the armies of the Arab States, under orders to march into Palestine on the day the Mandate ended.

WE APPEAL to the Jewish people throughout the Diaspora[17] to rally round the Jews of Eretz Israel in the tasks of immigration and upbuilding and to stand by them[18] in the great struggle for the realization of the age-old dream - the redemption of Israel.[19]

PLACING OUR TRUST IN THE ROCK OF ISRAEL, WE AFFIX OUR SIGNATURES TO THIS PROCLAMATION AT THIS SESSION OF THE PROVISIONAL COUNCIL OF THE STATE, ON THE SOIL OF THE HOMELAND, IN THE CITY OF TEL-AVIV, ON THIS SABBATH EVE, THE 5TH DAY OF IYAR, 5708 (14TH MAY, 1948)

*David Ben-Gurion*

| | | | |
|---|---|---|---|
| Daniel Auster | Eliyahu Dobkin | Zvi Luria | Abraham Katznelson |
| Mordekhai Bentov | Meir Wilner-Kovner | Golda Myerson | Felix Rosenblueth |
| Yitzchak Ben Zvi | Zerach Wahrhaftig | Nachum Nir | David Remez |
| Eliyahu Berligne | Herzl Vardi | Zvi Segal | Berl Repetur |
| Fritz Bernstein | Rachel Cohen | Rabbi Yehuda Leib Hacohen Fishman | Mordekhai Shattner |
| Rabbi Wolf Gold | Rabbi Kalman Kahana | David Zvi Pinkas | Ben Zion Sternberg |
| Meir Grabovsky | Saadia Kobashi | Aharon Zisling | Bekhor Shitreet |
| Yitzchak Gruenbaum | Rabbi Yitzchak Meir Levin | Moshe Kolodny | Moshe Shapira |
| Dr. Abraham Granovsky | Meir David Loevenstein | Eliezer Kaplan | Mosher Shertok |

---

[17]

**We appeal to the Jewish people throughout the Diaspora** (H. Leibman) As far as most of the Diaspora is concerned, Israel represents Judaism.

[18]

**And to stand by them** (Ahad Ha'am) Then from this centre the spirit of Judaism will go forth to the great circumference, to all the communities of the Diaspora, will breath new life into them and preserve their unity.

[19]

**We appeal to the Jewish people. . .the redemption of Israel** (Rav Eliezer Waldman) What we are doing here in redeeming the land of Israel is hastening the coming of the Messiah. It is a commandment of God to the Jewish people that we settle all the land of Israel. That means that as long as we don't have all the land, we are not going to be complete spiritually and total redemption will not be possible.

## Questions for Thought

1. Do you agree with Georges Friedman's comment (note #6) that the State of Israel is an "Israeli nation" but not a "Jewish State." What do you think he means by this?

2. How do you respond to comments such as those by Walid Khalidi (note #9) that the establishment of the State of Israel was done by "conquest."

## Exercise

List or categorize the major points contained in the Israeli Declaration of Independence. Compare these points with the points you listed in answering the exercise on page 49. How were they the same and different?

# Chapter 7
## What is the State of the Jews?

"...The State of Israel will be open for Jewish immigration and for the ingathering of the exiles; it will foster the development of the country for the benefit of all inhabitants; it will be based on freedom, justice, and peace as envisaged by the prophets of Israel; it will ensure complete equality of social and political rights to all its inhabitants irrespective of religion, race, or sex; it will guarantee freedom of religion, conscience, language, education and culture . . . " (Israeli Declaration of Independence)

When examining the "State" of the Jews, these sentiments should serve as important parameters.

In this chapter we will attempt to grapple with many of the issues relating to the essential character of the State of Israel. Many of the debates today revolve around conflicts of values: Peace, Democracy, The Land of Israel (*Eretz Yisrael*), The State of Israel (*Medinat Yisrael*), and The Jewish State. All of these terms carry a multiplicity of associations, and many of the passionate arguments in Israel, as well as in the diaspora, involve prioritizing "*ma kodem l'ma,*" what comes first.

On the following page are highlights of the original "Status Quo" agreement which outlined the principles by which the Jewish religion and Israeli democracy would live side by side. We will also look at Israel's Law of Return, which has been rightly described as the most Zionist law of the State of Israel. Finally, included in this chapter are reflections of various thinkers on the subject of religion and the State.

# The "Status Quo" Letter by David Ben Gurion

This letter was written by David Ben Gurion in his capacity as Chairman of the Jewish Agency Executive, to Rabbi J. L. Maimon, leader of the Agudat Israel in 1947:

The Executive of the Jewish Agency was informed by its Chairman of your request with regard to Personal Status Law, the Shabbat, Education and Kashrut in the future State of Israel. The Chairman of the Executive had already informed you that the Jewish Agency or any other body has not the authority to determine now the constitution of the future State. The establishment of the State needs the United Nations Resolution, and it is doubtful if freedom of conscience would not be guaranteed to all citizens. It is also important to make clear that our purpose is not to establish a theocracy. In the future Jewish State we shall also have non-Jewish citizens and it is our obligation to guarantee their equal rights, and not to use coercion to discriminate in religious or other matters. We were happy to hear that you understand that at this time it is impossible to have an authoritative body that will determine the future constitution, and that the future State will be free in certain matters to determine its constitution and the regime as will be decided by its citizens.

At the same time the Executive values your demands, and knows that they are a matter of concern not only to Agudat Israel but also to other Orthodox groups that are members of the Zionist Organization as well as to known partisans. The Executive understands your demand to be informed as to what is the Executive's attitude in those matters, and what it intends to do. The Executive invested the authority in the hands of the undersigned to respond to your demands on:

a.    **Shabbat:** It is clear that the official day of rest of the Jewish State will be on Shabbat; naturally the Christians and other religions will be granted the Shabbat on their days.

b.    **Kashrut:** All necessary steps will be taken to guarantee that any State kitchen for Jews will be kosher.

c.    **Personal Status Law:** The members of the Executive understand the importance of the question and the problems involved. All the bodies which are represented on the Executive will do all to satisfy the religious needs of the Orthodox, to prevent the division of the people.

d.    **Education:** The autonomy to the different educational systems (as now exists) will be guaranteed. No coercion from the authorities in matters of religion, and religious conscience will be applied. Naturally, the State will determine minimum studies in Hebrew, mathematics, history, etc., and will supervise them, but they will have the freedom to run the educational system according to their belief.

## The Law of Return[1]

The Law of Return embodies an expression of the Jewish and democratic nature of the State of Israel. The purpose of the Law of Return was to provide a solution to the Jewish people's problem - to establish a home for the entire Jewish people in Eretz Yisrael, the Land of Israel. In the Law of Return, the State of Israel put into practice the Zionist Movement's "credo" as pledged in the Declaration of Independence.

The Law of return declares that Israel constitutes a home not only for the inhabitants of the State, but also for all members of the Jewish people, whether living in countries where they were in distress, or living in countries of affluence.

The Law of Return declared both to the Jewish people and to the world that the State of Israel was in practice opening its gates to the Jews of the world to return to their ancient homeland.

It is impossible to understand the Law of Return, its name, and its significance, without stressing that the law was passed in 1950, in other words just five years after the end of World War II.

The Law of Return was enacted by the Knesset. It contains expressions pertaining to religion, history and nationalism, as well as to democracy, in a combination unique to Israel. It does indeed grant preferential treatment to Jews "returning" to their ancestral homeland.

In Israel, the debate has continued to rage over the Law of Return and how to proceed in this regard. Some wish to retain it as it stands, others want to modify it, while yet others point to the contradictions that exist between the preference for Jews and the value of equality, and therefore argue that the time has come to abolish the Law of Return.

In the opinion of this last group, although the law did indeed contribute to immigration and absorption when Israel was established, it is no longer needed. Abolishing the law would eliminate the preference accorded to Jews - even if they are citizens of another country - namely, that when they immigrate to Israel they are entitled to receive immediate Israeli citizenship.

---

[1] Adapted from material created by the Joint Authority for Jewish Zionist Education

Ever since its establishment, Israel has reiterated that it is a Jewish and democratic state. The Law of Return reflects the tension that exists in Israel between Israel's desire to be a Jewish state, a state of the entire Jewish people, and at the same time its desire to be a democratic state.

Discussion around the law and its wording constantly reappears on private and public agendas in Israel and the Diaspora. The Knesset has repeatedly debated proposals to amend the Law of Return, and it has indeed been amended a number of times over the years. These modifications reflect the changes that have taken place in Israeli society and the shifts taking place in political dialogue both inside Israel itself, as well as between Israel and the Diaspora. The present law also constitutes an expression of permanent trends, as well as of the Israeli legislative system's ability to adapt itself to changing circumstances.

The issue is also the focus of disagreement in dialogue with Diaspora Jewry, where it similarly draws attention to and intensifies differences in outlook. Many are dissatisfied with and wish to change the law's current wording. Others query whether the time has not come to repeal the law in order to minimize differences of opinion, avert new disagreements, and improve the State of Israel's democratic image in both domestic and foreign eyes.

An in-depth grasp of the issues is absolutely essential for Israeli students and Diaspora Jewry alike. Addressing the issues raised by the law is crucial to determining attitudes to this sensitive subject matter which is so fundamental to the nature and attributes of the State of Israel. Addressing the issues raised by the law is indispensable since what is involved constitutes a key theme in the political tension in Israel and the Diaspora.

The "Law of Return" was passed by the Knesset on July 6, 1950. It has also been amended twice. The first amendment (September 1, 1954) is underlined in the text below, while the second amendment (March 19, 1970) is italicized.

1.  Every Jew has the right to immigrate to the country.

2.  (a) Immigration shall be on the basis of an immigration visa.

    (b) An immigrant visa shall be issued to any Jew who has expressed a desire to settle in Israel, unless the Ministry of the Interior is satisfied that the applicant:

    (I) acts against the Jewish nation; or
    (ii) is liable to threaten the public health or security of the state; or
    (iii) has a criminal past which is liable to endanger the public's peace.

3.  (a) A Jew who has come to Israel and after his arrival expresses a desire to settle in the country may, while in Israel, obtain an immigrant certificate.

    (b) The exceptions specified in Article 2(b) shall apply to the issue of an immigrant certificate as well, though a person shall not be regarded as a threat to public health as a result of an illness which he has contracted after his arrival in Israel.

4.  Every Jew who has immigrated to the country before this law goes into effect and, every Jew who was born in the country, either before or after the law is effective, enjoys the same status as whoever immigrated on the basis of this law.

4A.  (a) *The rights of a Jew under this law and the rights of an immigrant under the Citizenship Law - 1952, as well as the rights of an immigrant under any other legislation, are also imparted on the child or grandchild of a Jew, and on the spouse of a Jew and on the spouse of the child or grandchild of a Jew; excluding a person who was a Jew and willingly changed his religion.*

    (b) *It is immaterial whether the Jew by virtue of whom the right is claimed under clause (a) is or is not alive and whether he did or did not immigrate to the country.*

    (c) *The reservations and conditions laid down with regard to a Jew or immigrant in this law, or under it, or in legislation as mentioned in clause (a) will apply to those who claim a right under clause (a) as well.*

4B.  *For the purpose of this law a "Jew" - anyone born to a Jewish mother or who has converted, and is not a member of another religion.*

The Ministry of the Interior is in charge of the enforcement of this law and may enact regulations in connection with its implementation and for the issue of immigrant visas and immigrant certificates to minors up to the age of 18.

*Regulations regarding clauses 4A and 4B require the approval of the Constitution, Law and Justice Committee of the Knesset.*

# REFLECTIONS

## Eliezer Schweid (1929 -     )
*Professor of Jewish Philosophy at the Hebrew University*

The State of Israel should regard itself a Zionist State, different from all other States, as the State of a people whose majority does not live within it.

Several conclusions follow from the above:

One -        Zionist policy expresses itself, practically, in attracting and absorbing Jewish immigrants.

Two -        Zionist policy must express itself in fostering the Jewish identity of the State as such, and of the people living within its borders.

Three -      Zionist policy must express itself in assuring that the State of Israel will concern itself directly with the fate of Jews living in exile, under oppressive condition.

Only a State responsible solely for the people living within its borders can allow itself the right to adopt a policy aimed at raising the standard of living within the framework of a "welfare state," whereas a state which is responsible for a nation whose majority does not dwell within its borders, may not allow itself the right to adopt such a policy, as an exclusive matter.

## Shmuel Hugo Bergman (1883 - 1975)
*Philosopher*

The State of Israel possesses the option to be a State like all other states with all the political intrigues, in which case it will lack importance and its basis will constitute an ordinary historical event, in which humanity will have no interest. Or perhaps, this little State will wish to serve as the genuine realization of Israel's age-old messianic vision - the beginning of a movement to improve the world along the lines of the Kingdom of Heaven. Only then will all the "earthly families" be blessed by the existence of the State.

Each day, every hour, the State of Israel will be tested as to whether it elected to pursue this path of the course of common politics. Each and every law will constitute a test. Even more, whatever will appear in books and newspapers in Israel, and whatever will be debated or asserted in Israel, will reflect whether we really wish to make our contribution or will satisfy ourselves with the ordinary patterns.

## Rabbi Maimon (1875 - 1962)
*Rabbi and leader of Religious Zionism*

The Religion and the State: The Hebrew State must be established and conducted in accordance with the principles of the Hebrew Religion, that is the Torah of Israel. Our conviction is clear: as far as we, the nation, are concerned, religion and state require each other.

## Rabbi I. Amital
*Rosh Yeshivat Gush Etzion*

Another form of Zionism also exists, the Zionism of redemption whose herald and great commentator was Rabbi Kook, of blessed memory. This Zionism did not emerge in order to solve the Jewish Question through the establishment of a Jewish State, but to serve as the Lord's vehicle for preparing Israel for its redemption. The habitation of the land of Israel by a group for its children, transforming its wasteland to gardens, and the establishment of independence within its borders, are stages in the process of redemption. Its internal objective is not the normalization of the Jewish Nation to be a nation like all nations, but to be a Holy People, the Nation of a Living God, whose center will be Jerusalem, sanctified by the presence of God's Temple. What we observe currently is the beginning of the prophetic vision of the redemption of Zion. These are the Messianic steps. And even though they are accompanied by suffering and tribulation, the strides are certain and the course is clear. For God favored Jacob and saved him from someone stronger. The time has come for Zionism to clear the way for the Zionism of Redemption even in our consciousness.

## Amnon Rubenstein (1931 - )
*Member of the "Meretz" political party*

"The State of Israel" is, at times, defined as a Jewish State. But this definition misses the mark. A State cannot be Jewish since it is not a creation of Judaism. From a religious viewpoint, a Jewish State implies a halachic state, one in which the Mosaic Torah is the only code of law, whereas from a free, liberal, non-halachic point of view, there is difficulty in attaching the term "Jew" to a State which is entirely a social and state instrument. It would be preferable, in my view, to return to Herzl's original definition: Israel is the State of the Jews . . . because it will be a state by virtue of its being A State of (belonging to) the Jews. Israel is duty-bound to preserve the basic Jewish moral lesson; what was hateful to us when we constituted a minority, what is bad for the Jews when they are scattered, will be hateful to us and harmful to us, even today, following our attainment of freedom and independence.

## Neturei Karta
*Ultra Orthodox Group*

What is the significance of the Zionist State which has emerged in our time? It signifies a denial of the basis of our faith. It asserts that the destiny and existence of God's people does not depend on the observance of the Torah and commandments, maintaining rather, that the Jewish nation will live by virtue of mortal strength and weaponry. The state signifies a denial of reward for fulfilling commandments and performing charitable acts and a denial of punishment for transgressions and violations of the Holy Torah, a flagrant denial of the original concepts of exile and redemption, namely, a disavowal of the belief that Israel's exile was a consequence of its sins – "And because of our sins we were exiled from our land" – and a denial of the belief that Israel's return to a state of freedom and government is contingent upon repentance and God's compassion, and that it will not come about by virtue of any power of earth, except by the hands of our just Messiah.

The Zionist State denies the Jewish people its essence and uniqueness, transforming it into a nation like all other nations, whose existence is not dependent upon the observance or abnegation of the Torah. The State before us was created as a substitute for the sanctity and Godliness of the People of Israel in order to transform its unique, deeply rooted essence into a territorial, gentile political one. The Zionist State represents total heresy uprooting the soul of our faith from its root and violating and covenant which God made with us in Horev.

## Uzzi Ornan (1923 - )

*Professor of Hebrew Language at the Hebrew University. One of the founders of the League to Prevent Religious Compulsion in Israel.*

It may be asserted that today it is clearer than ever that Israel is not a Jewish State. Three elements make it apparent that even before June '67, Israel was not a Jewish State.

Israel is not a state in which Jewish Law prevails. It possesses a sovereign legislature representing all the citizens of Israel, and only them. And it (the legislature) determines the laws of the state on the basis of its understanding and considerations, arrived at freely.

Israel is not a state which "belongs" to the Jews. Jews, in their respective lands, are not citizens of Israel. They do not participate in elections, nor in the government, and the obligation to render military service does not devolve upon them even during war time. Not all the millions of Jews throughout the world hopped on planes to rush to Israel as the war approached. And not only Jews demonstrated support and affection, contributing money and blood. And there were not even a few thousand Jews registered in the Israeli Consulates abroad as volunteer to join the IDF.

No person in Israel is obliged to be a Jew in order to be an Israeli. He can be a loyal citizen like any other citizen, and the war proved this convincingly. This was not a Jewish War but an Israeli War and these Israelis included citizens who are not Jewish. Many of them fell during battles and engagements, many contributed blood, many volunteered to assist on farms and other war efforts, and many were placed in hospitals during emergencies and tended the injured.

## The World Agudat Yisrael, Jerusalem (5715 - 5717, 1955 - 1957)

The aim of religious Judaism is that only the laws of the Torah shall be decisive in every aspect of life within the State. We are aware, however, that in light of the present composition of the population, the time for this has not come as yet. We have, therefore, presented a minimal program which will satisfy the chief requirements of religious Judaism and will foist nothing upon religious Jewry, and having received assurance that these basic requirements would be fulfilled, we found it possible to participate in the State's agencies. The attempt to foist a constitution upon us, a constitution which would contradict our principles, stands in opposition to the freedom of opinion and expression which you advocate. Therefore, there is no moral justification for demands made by proponents of a constitution. It would be preferable, therefore, that they legislate individual laws, and I emphasize that such laws, which will not be consistent with the spirit of the Torah, will be adjudged as temporary, by religious Judaism. In any case, better this than any attempt to foist a constitution upon us, one which would not be in accordance with the Torah.

## Muki Tsur
*Former Director-General of the United Kibbutz Movement*

One of the main achievements of Zionism is the absolute legitimization of secular life. The return of the Jew as a fully fledged player on the stage of national history has dictated a pluralism in which all forms of Jewish life, secular and religious can find expression.

## David Ben Gurion (1886-1973)
*First Prime Minister of Israel*

The religious debate in Israel is complicated by the peculiar character of the Jewish faith. The problem of religion in Israel is not similar to that of Church and State in Christian countries. The Jewish faith differs fundamentally from Christianity. It is not satisfied with abstract religious principles; it is based on mitzvot, on specific commandments as to what shall be done and what shall not be done, which comprehend the entire life of man from the moment of birth-and even earlier-until death and burial, leaving no neutral area outside the field of religion. At the same time the Jewish religion is national in character; it has absorbed all the historic elements in the life of the Jewish people from the time it came into being until this day. And it is not easy to separate the national from the religious aspect.

## Conservative Judaism
Selections from *Emet V'Emunah: Statement of Principles of Conservative Judaism*

The State of Israel is a unique phenomenon in history. On the one hand, it is and ought to be a democratic state which safeguards freedom of thought and action for all its citizens. On the other hand, it is and ought to be a distinctively Jewish state fostering Jewish religious and cultural values. Balancing the democratic and Jewish goals in Israeli society presents a constant challenge.

...We also believe that the essence of democracy is two fold: It expresses the will of the majority and scrupulously protects the rights of the minorities. Therefore, the laws passed by the State of Israel...should not be used to support a single religious view or establishment to the exclusion of others. The State of Israel, founded for the entire Jewish people, must in its actions and laws provide for the pluralism of Jewish life. The State should permit all rabbis, regardless of affiliation, to perform religious functions, including officiating at marriages, divorces and conversions.

...We believe that the State of Israel must encourage Jewish patterns of life in all of the agencies of the State and its political subdivisions. Without being a theocracy, Israel should reflect the highest religious and moral values of Judaism and be saturated with Jewish living to the fullest extent possible in a free society.

...While we strongly endorse the need to maintain the Jewish character and ambience of the State of Israel, we regard it as an overriding moral principle that ...the State... [not] employ coercion in the area of religious belief and practice.

...Both the State of Israel and Diaspora Jewry have roles to fill; each can and must aid and enrich the other in every possible way; each needs the other. It is our fervent hope that Zion will indeed be the center of Torah and Jerusalem a beacon lighting the way for the Jewish people and for humanity.

## Questions for Thought

1.  Is the Status Quo Agreement a reasonable basis for a solution to today's conflicts over religion and the State of Israel? What are its strengths and weaknesses?

2.  What are the implications of trying to change or abandon the Status Quo Agreement?

3.  Shmuel Bergman said that "The State of Israel possesses the option to be a State like all other states..." Do you feel that Israel can or should be a State like all others? Explain your answer.

4.  Since the destruction of the second Temple, Jews have been praying for the redemption of our People. What does Rabbi Amital mean by his idea of the Zionism of Redemption? What is your personal vision or understanding of Jewish redemption?

5.  Based upon the selections in this chapter, what potential do you see for agreement or compromise between non-religious and Orthodox Israelis? What are the barriers that you see to such agreement or compromise?

## Exercise

Make a list of ten elements that are unique to Israel as a Jewish State (as opposed to any other democratic state.) Next, rank them in order of importance.

1._____   2._____   3._____

4._____   5._____   6._____

7._____   8._____   9._____

10._____

## Exercise

Imagine if in the early years of the State of Israel Prime Minister David Ben Gurion would have invited *you* to make recommendations relating to the Jewish Character of the State of Israel. What would you have suggested? How would it be similar or different from the "Status Quo Agreement?"

# Chapter 8
## The Jewish People - Dare We Be One

On the 29 July 1806 in France Napoleon convened a Sanhedrin. This ultimate legislative body of the Jewish People had not met for some two thousand years since the destruction of the Second Temple.

The Jews in France were finally becoming beneficiaries of The Emancipation Process, which was to give equal rights to *all* citizens of the French Empire.

The Sanhedrin, made up of Rabbis and important Jewish notables, had the ominous task of responding to a series of questions. Among the questions addressed to the Assembly of Jewish notables were;

> *Do the Jews born in France, and treated by the law as French citizens, consider France as their country?*
>
> *Are they bound to defend it? Are they bound to obey the laws, and to follow the directions of the civil code?*

These questions signaled a redefinition of the relationship and responsibilities of French Jews to France in particular, and to the countries in the Empire in which Jews lived, in general. To a great extent we were being invited to "leave the Galut." We no longer had to live in "exile." Perhaps we should live "at home!"

In a sense from this time on, Jews have been grappling with this challenge and opportunity. We examined this dilemma previously in the chapter "Between Tel Aviv and New York" focusing on our relationship to our new "chosen" home. In this chapter we will review and analyze the relationship of the Jews in Israel to the Jews in the diaspora. What are the central issues to be discussed? What kind of ongoing relationship will emerge from these varying Jewish communities?

We are going to meet a number of thinkers, both from Israel and the diaspora, who have addressed these issues. Their reflections should help you grapple with the issues surrounding this dynamic relationship.

"It is time to say that America is a better place to be a Jew than Jerusalem. If there ever was a promised land, we Jewish Americans are living in it. Here Jews have flourished, not only in politics and the economy, but in matters of art, culture and learning. Jews feel safe here in many ways that they do not and can not in the State of Israel."

*Prof. Jacob Neusner* is a Professor of Religious Studies at the University of South Florida

---

"You want a Jewish State? Then please be so kind as to stand guard over it yourself. I've been doing it for dozens of years. Now it's your turn. Let's switch lives. You come here, serve in the army, worry about terror attacks, deal with the Orthodox, and shell out 50 percent of your income taxes, and I'll live in America, send you money, and visit you now and then, and criticize. Didn't you say we were partners? Then it seems to me a fair offer. I've given this project called Israel over forty years of my life. Why don't you give forty years of your life now, and I'll support you financially and politically. You can tell me what a crucial role I play in America, and I'll tell you how wonderful it is that you live in Israel."

*Matti Golan* is an Israeli journalist and author[1]

---

"It is the task of *Judaism*, rather than of Zionism as such, to supply the ideological, philosophical and theological foundations for Jewish existence throughout the world. Israelis will conduct the affairs of the State of Israel; Diaspora Jews will take responsibility for organizational and political matters in the Diaspora. However, all Jews should participate in articulating modes of positive Jewish attachment and involvement, finding ways to build the connections between Israel and the Diaspora, and among Jews around the world. We should seek to foster Jewish unity without insisting on uniformity, and to nurture the cultural, religious, and intellectual creativity of the Jewish people . . .

Predictions of ingathering as the natural reaction of the Jewish people to the establishment of the State have not materialized on the scale and for the reasons expected by some and hoped for by many more . . . Conventional Zionist explanations for the failure of *aliyah* from the West fail to comprehend the ties between Jews and their home countries . . . [For example], the relationship between American Jews and America needs to be seen as an affirmation of America, not a rejection of Israel.

*Rabbi David Gordis* is President of Hebrew College and Director of the Susan and David Wilstein Institute for Jewish Policy Studies[2]

---

[1] *With Friends Like You* by Matti Golan

[2] "Zionism, Israel and World Jewry: A Reappraisal," *Judaism* 39, 3 (Summer 1990)

How should we shape the relations between Israel and American Jewry? What do we want? And what can be expected? Most American Jews are not interested in aliyah . . . [I]t seems to me that there is a danger of a drifting apart between Israel and American Jewry, which may be caused by an estrangement from Judaism. Our common denominator is the Jewish roots of American Jewry. And if I were asked what should be the focus of our main efforts today I would say: to develop ways and means to strengthen the Jewishness of the Jews of the United States. Aliyah will be a consequence of the success in this area.

...[T]he time has come for us to consider not only what Jews in the diaspora can do for Israel, but what is the task of Israel vis a vis the Jewish communities. There are a number of things that I today consider to be essential:

1. To give full recognition to the realistic aspects of the situation; to be aware of our mutual dependence; and to realize that unless we foster these ties we shall undermine the basis of our existence.

2. To develop the potential inherent in the concept of the centrality of Israel which is today firmly rooted in the Jewish consciousness of most American Jews - as a complement to religion - in the preservation of Judaism.

3. Ways must be sought to strengthen the Jewish educational network. If we do not deal urgently with Jewish education - and I refer to the pre-university levels - we shall undermine the attachment of Jews to Judaism and the ties between Jewry and all Jewish affairs, including Israel.

4. Methods must be found for engaging American Jewry - in addition to aliyah - in Israeli and Jewish activities: economic, social, spiritual, and political.

It appears to me that in the American situation there is a basis for a broad network of relationships, which is essential for both sides. Israel is vital for the American Jew, for his status as an American and a Jew. For Israel, the preservation of American Jewry is vital.

*Yitzchak Rabin* is a former Prime Minister of Israel[3]

---

[3] Elan Levine, ed., "Shaping Relations, Strengthening Bonds," in *Diaspora - Exile - The Contemporary Jewish Condition* (New York: Steimatzky Shapolsky, 1986).

## Questions for Thought

1. Complete the following sentences:

   "It is better to be a Jew in America because _____."

   "It is better to be a Jew in Israel because_____."

2. If we choose not to live in Israel, what role do you feel we should play in Israel's life?

3. We often talk about our obligations as North American Jews to Israel. What obligations do Israeli Jews have to us?


## Exercise[4]

A. Mark the diagram which, in your opinion, expresses the existing relationship between Israel and the diaspora.

B. Mark the diagram which expresses the desired relationships between Israel and the diaspora.

D=Diaspora
I=Israel

_____

[4] Reprinted courtesy of Melitz

# Chapter 9
## Will the Real Israeli Please Stand Up?

After more than fifty years of Independence, Israel is an incredible mosaic of Jews from around the world. The creation of this new State to a great extent encouraged the creation of the new Jew, or the Israeli.

As we have seen from previous chapters, the desire and urgency to break from the past and establish new identities was an integral part of the Zionist Revolution. More than one hundred years later, is it in fact possible to speak of the new Israeli? Does such a phenomenon truly exist? Has the Israeli reality allowed for the maintaining of individual identities, or has the "melting pot" taken that away from the various communities for the "greater good" of the whole?

This chapter presents numerous Israeli characters, who reflect and relate to the most critical issues with which Israeli Society struggles, from their very individual perspectives. Such an exercise clearly involves stereotyping, none the less it is hoped that these characters present a window to understanding the complex dynamics of Israeli society.

After reading each of the "biographies," think about who you identify with most/least and why.

## Ultra Orthodox

Good day. My name is Yehuda Leib. I am named after my grandfather of blessed memory. I live in an area of Jerusalem called Meah Shearim. No doubt you have heard of it. My family has lived in this area for more than seven generations.

As you can see from the way I dress, our fashion sense hasn't really changed that much over the past two hundred years. Nor for that matter has much else.

Let me tell you about the way I live here in Eretz Yisroel. I want to be very clear from the outset. I live in the Land of Israel and not in the State of Israel. The establishment of the State is one of the major transgressions of our time; "Because of our sins we were exiled from our Land . . ." This is the opening of the Musaf Prayer for the Three Pilgrimage Festivals.

As such any move to change that situation, goes against the will of God. I live here because the Land of Israel is intrinsically Holy and we are commanded to live here. My family was here under the Turkish Empire, the British Empire, and unfortunately today, I live in this so called Jewish State under Israeli rule.

I wish to be in no position that would imply recognition of this tragic reality, and as such I do not vote in local, or National elections, nor will I, or my children serve in their army. Before the Zionists interfered with their colonial policies, there were no wars. True, there were occasional attacks, but we live in the Galut, exile which as I mentioned is a punishment.

I live strictly according to the Torah. I can confidently trace my roots back to Moshe Rabbenu. I am pretty convinced that he didn't look very different to the way I look. We resist change, because by it's very nature our Holy Torah accommodates itself to every situation.

I study at Yeshiva full time. Without constant study we cannot hope to know how to behave as God fearing Jews. This is the purpose of our lives. My wife, may she live long, teaches and helps to sustain the family. We have eight children with another on the way, please God.

You must come and visit us for a Shabbes, you will be more than welcome and then we could talk more.

## Religious Nationalist

Shalom, my name is Yehoshua Zion. I live in Bet El, north of Jerusalem, in the Shomron, an area unfortunately often referred to as "the Occupied Territories." If anything, they are being occupied by them. Unlike our friend Yehuda Leib, I believe that the establishment of the State of Israel is a miraculous event, integrally related to the process of our Redemption. The Messiah must be helped and by involving ourselves in the process we show ourselves worthy.

My Jewish Identity is based on three pillars: Eretz Yisrael (the Land of Israel), Am Yisrael (the people of Israel), and the Torah of Israel. The Land of Israel was promised to Abraham. It is ours. At present our firm belief of this fact is being challenged by the talks of returning or more giving away parts of the Land. This must never happen. I am a colonel in a tank unit. I have fought in too many wars and my love of this Land is too great to allow me to agree to any of these proposals.

Our spiritual leader is Rabbi Kook of blessed memory. He, unlike the majority of Orthodox Jews of his time, passionately believed in the religious significance of the return to Zion by Jews at the turn of this century. This was nothing less than the preemptive behavior bringing the Messiah. On Yom Haatzmaut (Israel's Independence Day) as on Yom Yerushalayim (the day celebrating Jerusalem's reunification after the Six Day War), we say the Hallel prayer with a blessing, for these days are festivals in every sense of the word.

The State of Israel is not just a State for the Jews. It must be an intrinsically a Jewish State. As such it should reflect Halacha (Jewish Law). Israel cannot possibly have what you would term, separation of church and state.

I strongly believe that all Jews should live in Israel, and I live my life with that hope.

With regards to the ongoing Peace process, I am of course deeply concerned. The hope for peace has captured the people of Israel throughout the ages, their blessing is peace, their prayers are for peace, and even when leaving for battle it calls out to its enemies for peace. But because of this very desire, we need great strengths of wisdom and courage not to mistake a deceitful peace for a real peace, a weak peace for a peace of honor and strength, a peace of crises and retreat for a peace of renewal and creation. We believe that the people will yet awaken from the illusion of this imaginary peace and will strengthen itself on its onward struggle.

We pray that this awakening will not be accompanied by sufferings or despair, but with brotherhood, honor and strength.

"May God grant His people strength. May He bless His People with peace."

## Secularist

Hi! My name is Talia, I live in North Tel Aviv, Ramat Aviv Gimmel, you may have heard of it as we have a show in Israel by that name. I have been asked to explain my Jewish Identity and way of life in Israel. To be honest, it is quite a strange request for me, as I do not see my identity as Jewish per se, but more as Israeli.

I have no relationship to the religion whatsoever. It performs a critical role in the Diaspora, maintaining an identity, but here in Israel, I think it is superfluous. Do not misunderstand me. I am very attached to many of the practices; On Friday night I light candles, (without a blessing) it is my decision not his. On Pesach the family gets together for dinner and celebrates freedom and the agricultural aspects of the Festival in a way that is really natural here in Israel. On Yom Kippur, I do not attend a Synagogue Service, instead I get together with close friends and contemplate where we are as a people living in the State of Israel. For many of us, Yom Kippur has taken on different meanings since the Yom Kippur War of 1973, many of my very close friends died in that war.

Every day I read, almost religiously, the newspapers. They are written in the same language as your prayers. I understand what I am reading . . . Do you?

Israel is, and must always be, a Democracy and as such religion must be the prerogative of the individual not of the State. In my mind there is far too much religious coercion and the democratic system is being compromised if not abused.

I attend numerous courses in Jewish Studies here in Tel Aviv, studying Tanach and Talmud. I of course have no interest in the legal aspects of these texts, I am fascinated by them because they are an integral part of my culture.

I have difficulty understanding why Jews today choose to live outside of Israel, I do not wish to tell anyone what to do or how to run their lives, nonetheless, it is a mystery.

I am very excited and also frustrated at the peace process. I am an active member of the Peace Now Movement. Its platform very much sums up my beliefs in this area; "The movement demands from any government in Israel that it maintain the traditional aims of Zionism, that it work toward a Jewish State and not one that negates the rights of some of its inhabitants; that does not rule over another nation; just as it would not allow another nation to rule over it . . . "

As an Israeli who is proud of her Jewishness, I believe that we of all peoples cannot strangle the nationalistic dreams and aspirations of another people. Certainly this has a price, but to me, better a land of peace than a piece of land.

## New Immigrant

My name is Amy. I made Aliyah just over a year ago from Chicago. I must tell you, it's been quite a journey. Of course it's great here and all that but . . . it's so different to what I expected.

I vividly remember my last Shabbat in the States, our Rabbi, gave me a special send off and when blessing me, she prayed that I find a community as warm and supportive as the one I was leaving. That's been a challenge To be a Conservative Jew in Israel isn't easy. Most Israelis have no idea as to my Jewish way of life, and many are confused why I chose to live here. Fortunately, here in Jerusalem there is a Masorti Synagogue and a wonderful community and it really does feel like home. But you know that is exactly the problem, everyone is so similar, there are hardly any native Israelis, it is almost as if we are a community apart. I want to be more accepted and more a part of the landscape. I think it is going to take time, but I believe that it will happen.

I must tell you there is never a dull moment out here. It is fast, dynamic, inspiring, frustrating, joyous and annoying, all of this very often at the same time!

There are immense challenges facing the State, be it the peace process, the economy, health services and improved education. You very much get pulled into the issues and from that point of view, the country seems small and very community conscious. I attend many demonstrations here, I am active in what is called the Peace Camp, and I also spend much time lobbying against the Conversion Bill. We, new immigrants from North America tend to stick out here but I firmly believe that we have a tremendous amount to give to this country - religious pluralism and greater accountability in the Government to name but a few.

You know what is really exciting, I can speak fluent Hebrew and understand the news and shows on T.V. I have made some good Israeli friends at work and they invite me to their family events as part of the family.

With all the frustrations I have no regrets, come and visit and see for yourselves.

אדון נכבד!

ביום א' ב' וג' אלול ש"ז יתאספו חו"צ בכל הארצות לקונגרס הציוני בבאזל (בשוייץ). והיום ההוא, שבו יתאחדו אחינו המפוזרים בדעה אחת, יהיה יום נצחון לתחזת לאומנו. האספה בבאזל תהיה התחלת תקופה חדשה בהתפתחות תנועתנו.

שם יספרו לנו אחינו מכל פנות הארץ ע"ד מצבם ומנמתיהם, שם יתברר מה, התנועה הציונית דורשת ממעריצה. שם תתרכז ותתאחד פעולתנו, שהיתה קרועה לכמה נזרים ע"י הדגה כוללת לכל סניפי העבודה. שם תראינה עינינו בבירור גלויות, שיאחד כל הכחות לפעולה אחת, גדולה וכבירה.

הקונגרס שואף למטרות קרובות ואפשריות. כל הדיעות האחרות על אדמתו קלוטות מן האויר. כל מעשי הקונגרס יהיו בפרסום גמור. בובחותינו ובהחלטותינו לא תהיה שום התנגדות לחוקי איזו ארץ ולהובותינו האזרחים. ביחוד אנחנו עדבים בזה, שכל מעשי האספה יהיו באופן מקובל ומדוצה להוי"ץ בדיסיא ולממשלתם הרוממה.

בזה נבקש אותך, אדון נכבר, ואת הברך שבהונגך, שתואילו לבא לבול ולהשתתף באספתנו. הקונגרס הראשון שלנו הוא החל שהבל פונים אליו, אוהבים ואויבים מחכים לו בעיים כלות, ולבן עלינו להראות לכל.בי חפצנו ברוד ויכלתנו גדולה. אם לא ימלא הקונגרס את תפקידו, או תבא ע"כ נסינה לאחור בתנועתנו לזמן רב. והכל תלוי רק בהשתתפות מרובה של אחינו ברוסיא, ששם רוב מנינינו.

אנו מקוים, שתדעו את חובתכם ותבאו לאספתנו באספה אפשר יהיה לדבר עברית. בבאזל יש אבסניא כסדה.

_____ בואך מהר נא להודיעע עפ"י הכתבת הנ"ל.

בשם "הועד להכנת הקונגרס הציוני":

Dr. Marcus Ehrenpreis      Dr. Theodor Herzl
המזכיר            ראש הועד

Buchdruckerei Max Rokne, Eisenstr. _____

An original invitation to the First Zionist Congress, held in Basle, Switzerland in 1897.

# Conclusion:
## Shnat Hayovel - Back to the Future

For much of this book we have been introspective, analyzing the factors which led to the reality which today we celebrate. We have reviewed history, grappled with ideologies and debated reality. In this the final chapter, we are going to leap back to the future.

How do we imagine Israel celebrating the next *Yovel* (50 years)? In much of our Jewish History we had to almost leave reality in order to make optimistic predictions about the future. We dreamed of Messianic times, to a large extent, because little in our daily lives led us to a brighter future. Many argue that the past one hundred years have been the most devastating, exciting and miraculous, in Jewish history. No other period has brought about such dramatic changes not only for the Jews, but for the world as a whole. Perhaps among the crowning achievements of this time is in our ability *as a people* to be in a position to carve our own future.

During this period, central phrases have captured the challenges facing the Jewish people:

At the end of the second World War; Survival
In the forties and fifties; Independence and Building
In the sixties and seventies; Identity
In the eighties and nineties; Continuity

**What do you think are going to be the key phrases in the 21$^{st}$ century?**

_____     _____     _____

**EXERCISE**

**On the following page is the translated text of the invitation to the First Zionist Congress in Basle, Switzerland in 1897. Write an invitation to an International Zionist Congress to be held in 2048, on Israel's 100th year. What will be on the agenda? Do you think it will be easy to persuade people to come?**

_____

_____

_____

_____

Dear Sir!

On Sunday, Monday and Tuesday of this year Lovers of Zion from all lands will assemble for the Zionist Congress in Basel (Switzerland). That day, on which our dispersed brethren will unite in agreement, will be a day of victory for the resurrection of our nation. The gathering in Basel will be the beginning of a new period in the development of our movement.

There it will become clear what the Zionist Movement demands of its admirers. There we shall behold a Gathering of the Diaspora which will unite al our groups for concerted and historic action. The Congress strives for attainable goals.

We hereby request, distinguished sir, that you and those in your circle will kindly join us in Basel and participate in our gathering. Our first Congress is the "summit toward which all face" (from the Talmud). Friends and foes alike will have their eyes upon us. Hence we must show all that our will is clear and our ability is great. If the Congress will not fulfill its purpose, our movement will suffer a great setback. And everything depends upon participation.

We hope that you will recognize your obligation and attend. At the gathering it will be possible to speak Hebrew. (In Basel there is a kosher hotel.)

In the name of the Planning Committee of the Zionist Congress:


*Dr. Theodore Herzl*      *Dr. Marcus Ehrenpreis*

Head of Committee      Secretary